RESOURCES OF MUSIC HANDBOOKS

Music in the Primary School

RESOURCES OF MUSIC HANDBOOKS

Music in the Primary School

Revised for the 1995 National Curriculum

JANET MILLS

CAMBRIDGE
UNIVERSITY PRESS

PUBLISHED BY THE PRESS SYNDICATE OF THE UNIVERSITY OF CAMBRIDGE
The Pitt Building, Trumpington Street, Cambridge, United Kingdom

CAMBRIDGE UNIVERSITY PRESS
The Edinburgh Building, Cambridge CB2 2RU, UK   www.cup.cam.ac.uk
40 West 20th Street, New York, NY 10011–4211, USA   www.cup.org
10 Stamford Road, Oakleigh, Melbourne 3166, Australia
Ruiz de Alarcón 13, 28014 Madrid, Spain

© Cambridge University Press 1991

First published 1991
Second edition, revised for the National Curriculum 1993
Third printing, revised for the National Curriculum 1995
Sixth printing 1999

Printed in the United Kingdom at the University Press, Cambridge

A catalogue record for this book is available from the British Library

ISBN 0 521 44825 5 paperback

Acknowledgements

The Publishers would like to thank the following for permission to
use extracts from material in their copyright:

Association of Professional Music Therapists, extract on p. 114 from
Music Therapy in the Education Service; Calouste Gulbenkian
Foundation, extracts on pp. 140, 141; Sybil Marshall, extract on
p. 84 from *An Experiment in Education* (CUP), and C. Davies, extract
on p. 102 from *British Journal of Music Education* (CUP); Sally Crane
for her poem 'The Runaway Seed', on p. 66; Sally Crowther for her
poem 'The Sea', on p. 39; Faber and Faber Ltd, extract on p. 74 from
Hans Keller *Criticism*; HMSO, extracts on pp. 1, 59, 67, 71, 72, 117,
118, 146–47; this material is reproduced with the permission of the
Controller of Her Majesty's Stationery Office; Hutchinson, extract on
p. 53 from J. M. Corredor *Conversations with Casals*; International
Society for Music Education, extracts on pp. 102–103 from Roger
Buckton's article in A. Kemp *Research in Music Education*, and on
pp. 25 and 131 from William Salaman's article in the *International
Journal of Music Education*; John Murray (Publishers) Ltd, extract on
p. 11 from John Betjeman's *Summoned by Bells*; Marion Boyars
Publishers Ltd London/New York, for permission to use extracts from
Silence: Letters and Writings by John Cage; National Curriculum
Council, extract on p. 2; Oxford University Press, extract on p. 57
from Iona and Peter Opie *The Singing Game*, and on p. 127 from
D. Arnold *The New Oxford Companion to Music*; Ronnie Scott, for the
quote on p. 150; Routledge, extracts on pp. 109–10 from
K. Swanwick *Music, Mind and Education*; Society for Research in
Psychology of Music and Music Education, extract on p. 57 from
article by Graham Welch in *Psychology of Music*; Keith Swanwick
and June Tillman for Fig. 7 on p. 98; TES extract on p. 5 from an
article by Letwin; and the University of Exeter School of Education,
extract on p. 1 from Addison *Beyond Music*.

Contents

About the author

Janet Mills read music and mathematics at the University of York, and took a PGCE at the University of Leeds. She then became Head of Music at The Holy Family School in Keighley, and later at Brighouse Girls' Grammar School. Following DPhil research at the University of Oxford, based on work in primary and secondary schools, she was appointed to Westminster College to work with primary and secondary teachers and student teachers. She moved to the University of Exeter in 1988, where she worked with BA(Ed) and PGCE primary students, and teachers taking in-service courses and higher degrees. Her time as a teacher educator was divided between those who specialised in music and those who chose to specialise in other subjects.

Foreword

Time was when most application forms for teaching posts in primary schools included the question 'Do you play the piano?' It usually came right at the end; you were never quite sure why. Was it an afterthought – suggesting that music had no great significance in the curriculum, but it would be useful to have someone who could play the hymns for assembly? Or was it a last, desperate cry from the heart – 'We hardly dare mention this, but if you should just happen to play the piano that would be marvellous. You can take every class for singing, and you can organise the Christmas concert, and play for country dancing; and, because you obviously know how to read music, you can teach recorders and organise a percussion band . . . and . . . and . . .' Someone who could play the piano was the answer to many a headteacher's prayers.

In the expectation that only a minority of applicants would answer that question in the affirmative, schools looked to the teacher training colleges (as they were then called) to put on 'curriculum courses' that would equip teachers to cope with their own class music lessons. But here again, the norm against which the course content was measured was still the accomplished piano-playing teacher; in some way students were to be brought as close as possible to that ideal, even though the time allocated was not normally more than a few hours a week across a single academic year. Lecturers tried hard to encourage and inspire, and students – beginner pianists, elementary recorder players, first-position violinists – laboured bravely to reach worthwhile standards and to acquire repertoires for singing and music appreciation lessons. But the one thing such curriculum courses could not guarantee to deliver was the confidence needed to teach music.

Janet Mills assumes that 'Music is for all teachers' but she does not assume that every teacher has to be a pianist. The strength of her argument is its realistic approach; there must be something that everyone can do. But confidence is paramount. Accepting that music now has a high priority in primary schools and is endorsed by the National Curriculum, this book sets out a comprehensive scheme that really can be organised and taught by the generalist teacher. No longer do we regard music in schools as icing on the cake; and it should now be clear that few people are better placed than primary school class teachers to see that musical experience becomes, from the start, a truly important part of every child's education.

John Paynter

ix

Author's acknowledgements

I wish to thank all the teachers and student teachers who helped with the development of this book. I owe a special debt of gratitude to Karen Brock, Sally Crane, Sally Crowther, Poppy Hughes, and Wendy Reynolds.

David Acheson and Jennifer Buckham took the photographs, and I would like to thank Miss Winifred Pope, Headteacher at Wantage CE Junior School, and Miss Eileen Mann, Acting Headteacher at SS Mary and John CE First School, Oxford, for permitting those photographs to be taken in their schools.

Last, but far from least, the children. Some appear in case studies, and others in photographs.-But many more have, sometimes unwittingly, played their part in the development of my ideas. I wish to thank them all.

Primary teachers and music

'I am more concerned for the future of the human race than I
am for the future of music.'
    Richard Addison in *Beyond Music* (Addison, 1988: 13)

'Music education should be mainly concerned with bringing
children into contact with the musician's fundamental
activities of performing, composing and listening.'
    HM Inspectorate in *Music from 5 to 16* (DES, 1985a: 2)

Music in primary schools

I start by outlining my view of the place of music in primary
schools. Like Richard Addison, I think that music education has more
to do with the education of children than the transmission of some
musical heritage. Like the writers of *Music from 5 to 16*, I think of music
education as an active experience in which children compose, perform
and listen.

Not all activities that sometimes pass for music in primary school
are, in my terms, music. Drawing a flute is not music, though it might
be an appropriate artistic activity for children who have just performed
the musical activity of listening to a flute being played. Reading about
the life of Mozart is not music, though it could be a useful language
exercise for children who have listened to a piece by Mozart, and who
want to find out more about his life. Making a musical instrument is not
music, though playing it may be.

The activities of composing, performing and listening are fundamental to musicianship, and practice in them may result in some pupils
choosing careers as composers, performers or critics. But I do not
engage children in composing, performing and listening out of any
vocational motive – rather because I want the children to grow through
music. All children can grow through music, so music education is for
all children.

As music is for all children, the music curriculum must be
determined in response to individual musical need. No single blanket

1

programme will be suitable for all children, any more than it would be in mathematics or English. No special group – for instance those, sometimes referred to as gifted, who will become able performers – has any higher claim on the music curriculum. All children have an equal right to an appropriate music education.

Music is for all teachers. I mean by this that children ideally do music with their class teacher, not a specialist teacher who sees them only for music. At present, many primary schools employ music specialists to take responsibility for the music of several classes. This contrasts with practice in all other curriculum areas where classes are taught usually by class teachers on the grounds that the advantages of having a teacher who knows you outweigh those of being taught by someone with particular specialist expertise. If this is true of other areas, why is it not true of music? In practice, music is often perceived as being different because music teachers are assumed to need skills that it would be unreasonable to expect all teachers to possess. Music lessons are sometimes organised rather like rehearsals of choirs and orchestras, with the teacher conducting, playing the piano, and demonstrating on a range of instruments, including her singing voice. In this sort of lesson, the teacher does need to be in musical control. But as we shall see later, there is no need to organise music lessons like this. Just as we can develop children's written language without being a novelist, it is perfectly possible to engage children in music without being a pianist. Of course, having specialist music skills is useful to teachers, and schools will still need teachers who can play the piano, direct choirs, and so on. But there is no need for these people to do all the music teaching in the school. Class teachers, given appropriate preparation and support, are all capable of teaching music. This way, music takes its place as part of the whole primary curriculum. Children and teachers make day-to-day links between work in music and other curriculum areas. Class teachers who anyway 'accept full responsibility for . . . the progress in learning of each pupil in the class' (National Curriculum Council, 1989: 13), will know their pupils' musical progress at first hand.

Finally, music in the primary school must be an activity that is pleasurable for both children and teachers. I do not mean to suggest that music should be organised solely as entertainment, or that the atmosphere in a music lesson should always be akin to that of a party. In any case, that would be unlikely to result in pleasure for the teacher. I mean that the process of working as a musician – by composing, performing and listening – must be enjoyable if it is to have any value.

Similarly, the business of facilitating the musical activity of children must be pleasurable and satisfying for the teacher. Music lessons that become boring, which degenerate into disciplinary incidents, or which culminate in the teacher haranguing the class about extra-musical matters such as holding books properly, paying attention, and sitting up straight, are worse than useless. Children who repeatedly attend this sort of music lesson become disenchanted with music long before they enter secondary school. Of course there will be moments in music lessons when a child has to be reprimanded. There will be occasions when children must be encouraged to increase the standards they set for their work in music. This might even mean asking children to revisit work they rather hoped was finished. But music should be something we engage in because we feel better for it. It should never become a mere duty, for teachers or pupils.

In short, music is

o   an active subject consisting of the activities of composing, performing and listening
o   for all children
o   for all teachers
o   fun.   – find a balance

Primary music teachers

I have said that music is a subject for all teachers. Yet there are, at present, many primary teachers who do not teach music. Indeed, music is the subject in which children are most frequently taught by someone other than their class teacher.[1] It is also the subject that fewest teachers think they need to be able to teach.[2] Does this mean that music is a low priority in primary school? Hardly. Many primary schools go to the trouble of appointing special music teachers.[3] Advertisements for primary posts refer to music more frequently than any other subject.[4] The point is that the special music teachers tend to operate in different ways from teachers with curriculum responsibility in any other subject. Whereas mathematics curriculum leaders, for instance, often operate mainly as co-ordinators of the school mathematics curriculum, and as advisers to their generalist colleagues, music curriculum leaders are more likely to take over the music of several classes, whilst their own teachers are busy elsewhere. In other words, music curriculum leaders tend to operate as specialists, not as consultants.

The idea of generalist music teaching is not a new one. The Plowden Report (CACE, 1967) came out in favour of it almost thirty years ago. So why is music still so often taught by specialists? There are, I think, two main, linked, reasons. First, many generalists lack confidence in their ability to teach music. Second, many music curriculum leaders have not developed an ability to raise the confidence of generalists. In other words, these curriculum leaders have not learnt to act as consultants to generalists without specialist music skills.

Most primary teachers received their primary music teaching at the hands of music specialists who displayed formal skills such as piano playing and conducting. Today's music specialists are also able to draw on these skills when they wish to help children achieve a musical objective. There are, as we shall see, hardly any situations in which display of these skills is crucial to children's success; teachers usually have a number of options concerning their teaching style. Specialists use specialist skills out of habit or preference, not necessity. But because they often appear to use these skills as a matter of course, their performance can seem intimidating and unachievable to outsiders. Primary music can seem to be about the demonstration of teacher skill, not the promotion of child learning.

Generalists often arrive at their professional training with a well-established low confidence in their ability to teach music. I found music to be the subject which most worried a group of generalist student teachers (Mills, 1989a). Many student teachers attribute their low confidence to an inability to emulate the teaching style of the music teachers they remember from their own primary education. They speak of what they perceive to be their own musical inadequacies; perhaps they do not play the piano, or perhaps they are not confident singers. Often, sadly, they first decided that they were inadequate as musicians when a primary teacher criticised their musicianship. The story most frequently told is one of rejection from a junior school choir.

These students measure their musical competence by what they cannot do. Measurement of what they *can* do would be more to the point. Every student teacher I have met is able to do a great deal. Nearly all enjoy listening to some particular styles of music. Many have some experience of playing one or more instruments, perhaps by ear. These are musical activities which can be shared with children, and from which new skills and interests grow. But students and teachers bring much more than their music skills to their music teaching: they bring their teaching expertise. The teaching skills that teachers use to

4

facilitate children's learning in mathematics, English, and so on, can be applied to music too. Music teaching is not about teachers performing to children; it is about children learning. Performing to children is only one way of helping children to learn. There are many situations in which other teaching techniques are equally, if not more, effective.

Although many primary students lack confidence in music, others have no such worries. Perhaps they have taken piano lessons for some years, or achieved an A-level in music. They may be studying music as a main subject within a B Ed, or may have entered a PGCE course on completion of a music degree. Such students have a head-start over their colleagues. This is not just because they have skills which the rest lack; there are ways of getting round that. Their advantage is that they already have musical self-esteem. They can make positive statements about their abilities and achievements as composers, performers and listeners. They may feel that the pattern of their musical development has been uneven. Perhaps they have specialised in performing at the expense of composing, or perhaps their listening experience has been narrow. But they know that they start music teaching from a position of some strength.

We seek to develop musical self-esteem in the children we teach. We want children to feel satisfaction when they achieve something worth while. The view that children with self-esteem achieve more, and that the relationship is, to some extent, causal, underpins much contemporary educational thought. The GCSE and Records of Achievement are just two initiatives that formalise the view that children accomplish more when encouraged to think positively about their strengths and achievements, whilst remaining sensitive to the possibility of further development. The GCSE purports to measure what children know, understand, and can do. The progressive development of Records of Achievement involves children in frequent reflection on their strengths. Failure motivates but rarely. The small number of educational commentators who, during the late 1980s, supported proposals to administer national tests to children from the age of 7, and then tell them how well or badly they had done on the grounds that children '. . . had better learn from the earliest possible age to come to terms with their own capabilities . . .' (Letwin, 1987: 112), found themselves without the general support of the wider educational community.

If self-esteem is good for children, then it seems likely that it is good for teachers teaching music. Teachers with musical self-esteem can, like those who help children compile their Records of Achievement, enable less confident colleagues to develop it. First, they can tackle the matter head on. They can encourage colleagues to list their skills, and help them to develop approaches to music teaching that they feel ready to try. Second, they can show, through at least occasional demonstration of teaching approaches within the reach of generalist colleagues, that it is possible to teach music without recourse to specialist skills. This means thinking about the options that teachers have when deciding how to help children to achieve a musical objective, and not always making a specialist selection.

Teachers under stress can revert to teaching as they were taught, whatever the content and approach of their teacher training. As most teachers are the product of a specialist system of primary music teaching, this is an obstacle to the development of generalist music teaching. Faced with a colleague who is worried about teaching music, a music curriculum leader may be tempted to teach the class personally, rather than help the other's development in music teaching. This does not promote the development of the generalist's self-esteem. Nor does it develop musical self-esteem in the children involved, for they become aware that music cannot be handled by everyone. Through music consultancy, rather than specialist music teaching, a more positive cycle of musical confidence can be generated. Children become the teachers of tomorrow. The musical self-esteem of teachers will, progressively, rise.

Music is, as we have seen, a subject of extremes. It has most specialist teachers, is taught by fewest class teachers, and is the subject in which most students feel least confident. But it is far from a doomed subject. What we need to do is to channel the abilities of all those specialists away from perpetuating the myth that primary music can be taught only by those like them, and towards the development of more generalist music teaching.

Towards music teaching

Up to now we have concentrated on the importance of all teachers learning to lead musical activities with children. But activities alone do not make a curriculum. We need to think also about the aims and purposes of music teaching, and about balance, progression, and evaluation. We must consider the relationship of music to the whole primary curriculum, and the role of music within the life of the school.

In other words, we need some sort of theoretical framework for our teaching. I take the view that the idea of a framework makes more sense when teachers already have experience of leading musical activity. The structure of this book reflects this view. The development of a theoretical framework is left until Part Two. In Part One, the focus is on the organisation of music making. Aims, planning and preparation, evaluation, progression, links with other subjects, and so on, are addressed only on a day-to-day level. The context of this music making is simply a music curriculum which is active, for all, and fun. There is an emphasis on the variety of approaches which teachers of differing taste and experience may use to involve children in music making. Part One is, in a sense, teacher-centred.

Part Two is more child-centred. Following a chapter on aspects of children's development in music, the subject of curriculum planning is addressed. Music is then set within the primary curriculum and, finally, within the primary school. No single framework for primary music could suit all schools or teachers. Much depends on the participating children and teachers, the school ethos, prevailing LEA and DFE policies, and so on. Consequently, I do not provide any blueprints. The information here is intended to help teachers develop their own framework, and to design and implement a curriculum that fits their particular circumstances.

The whole of this book is addressed to all teachers. There is no special section for generalists, nor one for music consultants. Initially, the needs of generalists and consultants may differ in emphasis. Generalists starting to teach music may at first be preoccupied with finding activities with which they can cope. Other readers may be concerned more with developing their range of teaching approaches, with curriculum development, or with other long-term issues. But even the most hesitant generalists soon become able to take significant personal responsibility for their music teaching. The relationship between generalists and consultants in music stabilises to become no different from that in other subjects. Both generalists and consultants become involved in the development and implementation of school music policy. So all teachers will, eventually, want to think about the matters dealt with in Part Two.

Whenever possible, I avoid the use of musical jargon. Where inclusion of a term which may be unfamiliar to some readers seems unavoidable, its first appearance is accompanied by a few words of explanation. Staff notation – sometimes called stave notation or

7

conventional music notation – does not appear at all. Many teachers can read music, or are learning to do so. But a book that contains staff notation is impenetrable to those who cannot already read it fluently. Since much primary music – possibly all – can be taught effectively without recourse to staff notation, there is no point in including it here. Teachers who do read music will have no difficulty in seeing how to apply this skill to their teaching, when they feel that this is appropriate.

Writing a book which is accessible to all teachers has involved careful choice of language, but no compromise of musical or educational purpose. There is nothing second-best about a properly organised and supported system of generalist music teaching.

8

Starting-points for Musical Activity

Music consists of the interrelated activities of composing, performing and listening. The interrelation has two main components. First, much music making involves musicians in doing two, or even three, of these activities simultaneously. When listening to music, we may respond by performing, for example clapping in time with the beat. When performing, we listen to what we are playing. When composing, we often try out ideas by performing them, and make judgements about them as a result of listening. Second, the three activities have a common factor: they are all creative. Creativity is not just an attribute of composers. Performers are not automatons concerned exclusively with accuracy; their interpretation of a composition reflects their personal style. Listeners are not just pieces of blotting paper; they have differing, personal, responses to the same performance.

But despite the interrelation, we can think of music as a sequence of creative process

composing → performing → listening

which can be entered at any of three stages. At the first stage of this sequence we have composers, who devise music. They may also, simultaneously, perform and listen. At the second stage we have performers, who interpret music which is already composed. They may also be listening. At the third stage we find listeners, who listen to the performance of others. They are not, at that moment, either composing or performing. In general, I have organised the musical activities in Part One according to where children are entering this sequence. Activities in which children devise music are found in chapter 3, *Composing*. This is followed by chapter 4, *Performing*, which focuses on the interpretation of music that has already been composed. Finally, chapter 5, *Listening*, deals with activities in which children enter the sequence as members of an audience.

In each chapter I draw attention to a range of possible approaches to teaching music. Teachers new to music can start with approaches that they find comfortable, although they should be aware that they are making a choice, that others might choose differently, and that they may wish to choose differently themselves on a later occasion. More experienced music teachers may wish to explore less familiar approaches in a more systematic way.

But before getting involved in composing, performing and listening *per se*, we take a look in chapter 2 at an educationally valuable form of music making which can include any, or all, of the three activities, and which can serve as an effective introduction to class music for teachers: music games.

CHAPTER TWO

Music games

'The dread of beatings! Dread of being late! And, greatest dread of all, the dread of games!'
John Betjeman, in *Summoned by Bells*, VII: Marlborough
(Betjeman, 1960: 67)

John Betjeman was not referring to music games. There is, so far as I am aware, nothing dreadful about music games. Quite the contrary. Children find them fun, and so do teachers, even those who are very worried about teaching music. In music games, there is often little need for the teacher to do anything musical at all. In some games, the teacher needs only to explain the game, tell the children when to start, and observe them whilst the game takes its natural course. In others, the teacher will be involved as a musician, but will be able to set him- or herself musical tasks substantially easier than those being presented to the children. In any case, the structure of the game is used to manage the development of the activity. Inexperienced teachers do not then find their carefully organised lesson plans disintegrating around them as a child responds to a task in a seemingly inexplicable manner. The teacher and children have met together to play a game, and that is what they do.

Music games must, of course, have some musical purpose. This means that they must involve children in at least one of the three processes of listening, performing, composing. And if they are to form a useful part of a progressive music education, games must enable us to observe something about the children's abilities or needs as composers, performers or listeners. So there are two musical questions to be asked about the games we consider:

1 What composing, listening, or performing are the children doing? (*Musical process*)
2 What can the teacher learn about the children's musicianship? (*Musical assessment*)

11

And because primary teachers teach children for the whole curriculum, not just music, there is a third question:

3 What else can the teacher learn about the children? (*General assessment*)

We shall return to these questions when we consider activities other than games.

The games here are described in more detail than most of the other activities. This is because many readers of this chapter may be inexperienced in music teaching, though experienced in teaching other areas of the primary curriculum. I want to illustrate some points that underpin music and music teaching. These include the following:

1 **Music cannot be rushed.**
   Time is one of the raw materials of music. You cannot listen to, or perform, a piece on 'fast forward'.

2 **Pattern in music cannot be perceived unless it is sustained.**
   This point is linked to the previous one. It takes time, and repetition, for a pattern to be recognised as such. Recognising pattern helps us to make sense of music.

3 **Though hearing is the dominant sense in music, the other senses are important too.**
   Sight and sound often act together in the co-ordination of music, for instance in conducting. Touch, and memory of touch, are crucial to some forms of performing. Any sensory experience may act as a stimulus for composition.

4 **Making mistakes, and recovering from them, is a crucial component of performing.**
   Even the most accomplished performers make mistakes. Children need to learn to recover from their mistakes, and those of others; a performance need not be stopped whenever something goes wrong.

5 **Group music making is shared.**
   Performers support and help each other; they are not in competition.

6 **Extraneous sound can detract from music.**
   Music is a function of sound in time. Competing sound, such as that of the teacher's voice, can interfere with musical perception and appreciation.

12

7   **Music comes in a variety of styles.**
    In particular, music need have neither a recognisable melody, nor
    a regularly repeating pulse.

Music games can be used in many ways. As warm-up activities,
they can capture children's interest, and focus their attention at the
start of a substantial music lesson. As fill-in activities, they can act as
freestanding mini music lessons. Some can eliminate the tedium from
repetitive learning. As co-operative activities, they can promote the
development of bonding within a class, and between a class and their
teacher. But here we consider the games as activities in their own right.

Music games come in a variety of forms. Three types are included
here:

o   Classroom music games
o   Traditional music games
o   Music games with borrowed structures

Readers may find it helpful to try out some games with children before
moving on to subsequent chapters.

Classroom music games

These are music games that have been devised specifically for
classroom use. Two contrasting games are described here: *Switch* and
Conductor. Both of these games, in various versions, are frequently
played in classrooms, and both can be found in other books.[1] The
version of *Switch* suggested here is an adaptation of the published
version.

Switch

Switch is suitable for full classes, or smaller groups. It is a
structured copying game enjoyed by children of any primary age, but it
is described here with juniors in mind. Though some children become
confident enough to lead *Switch*, it is perhaps best if the teacher first
introduces it. Sit with the children in a circle and explain the game like
this: 'I am going to perform some patterns. Join in with me. When I
change patterns, you change too.' Without saying anything else, start
clapping your hands regularly, at a comfortable pace (perhaps two
claps a second). Once the children have all joined in, move to another
simple pattern – perhaps slapping your lap at the same pace. When the

13

children change from clapping to slapping, you know that they have understood the game, and are ready to try some more patterns. Stay on each pattern long enough for children to feel the repetition in what they are doing – at least fifteen seconds for easy patterns, and longer for more complicated ones – and move continuously between patterns so that the beat is maintained and the whole game becomes a continuous piece of music. Try to choose patterns that all children can join in with accurately after a few tries, but if you happen to choose a pattern which one or more children cannot manage, do not persist with it, but move to another, easier, pattern to get the group back together again. In an introductory game of *Switch*, it is probably best to include a sequence of at least eight patterns drawn from the following categories:

Simple regular patterns at the same pace as the introductory clapping

Instead of clapping, stamp one or both feet, for instance.

Complex regular patterns, still at the same pace

Instead of clapping repeatedly, try **clap-clap-slap-clap, clap-clap-slap-clap** or **clap-clap-click, clap-clap-click**. (I have never learned to click my fingers, but this is not a problem. Children realise what I am trying to do, copy my gesture, and supply a click as well. However, I understand that teachers who *can* click occasionally meet children upset because they *cannot*! One teacher resolves this by supplying a mouth click simultaneously with the finger click. Perhaps there are advantages in being a non-clicking teacher . . .)

Simple regular patterns at a half or a quarter of the pace of the introductory clapping

Try standing up for a count of four claps and then sitting down for another four, or placing your hands on the floor for a count of two claps, then on your lap for another two.

Irregular patterns

You might clap the rhythm of 'Polly put the kettle on', or 'We'll all have tea' from the end of the same nursery rhyme. If the children find that easy, try replacing the clap for 'tea' with a slap.

14

It is best not to spoil the impression of *Switch* as a continuous piece of music by giving the children any verbal instructions once it has started. End the game by folding your arms, or resting your hands on your lap. The children copy, and the game finishes.

What is the musical purpose of *Switch*? Let us refer back to the three questions on pages 11–12:

1   What composing, listening, or performing are the children doing? (*Musical process*)
2   What can the teacher learn about the children's musicianship? (*Musical assessment*)
3   What else can the teacher learn about the children? (*General assessment*)

In *Switch*, the children's main role is as performers. They are taking part in a piece of music composed by the leader. They perform by recognising, and repeating, patterns in the composition. Repeating of patterns helps children to learn how to anticipate sounds, and the movements that cause them: an important aspect of performance. In the spirit of the game, the children make an effort to recognise each pattern as soon as possible – thus increasing their skill in pattern recognition. As they repeat patterns, they develop their physical co-ordination, so are likely to be able to perform even better in the future. As well as performing, the children are listening. Sight is important in this game too, and many children rely on *seeing* the pattern. During *Switch*, teachers can become aware of the differing abilities of children in these performing skills. The gross body movement involved makes it relatively easy to spot children with difficulties in pattern recognition or physical co-ordination. Pattern recognition underpins learning in other subjects too. A child who seems to lack it in *Switch* merits investigation of pattern recognition in mathematics and art, for instance.

Is *Switch* just a one-off activity, or is there some value in playing it on several occasions? Of course children will become bored if they are forever playing *Switch* – particularly if the patterns are too easy, or impossible. But *Switch* can be developed in a number of ways to musical purpose. Here are three suggestions.

1   **Making *Switch* more difficult**
    Switch would be more challenging if one spent less time on each pattern. But this would be at the expense of some of the musical

A group of 10-year-olds follow their teacher in a game of *Switch*. Note the
extent to which they are *seeing* the pattern.

value of the game, for children would no longer have the musical
experience of participating in repeating rhythmic patterns. Instead, try clapping some more challenging patterns, such as a line
from *Ring a Ring o' Roses* or *Humpty Dumpty Sat on a Wall*. Next,
you could use mixed body sounds to convey these rhythms. Or you
might prefer to make up some patterns of the length you want. The
patterns can be as complicated as you like, provided that you can
sustain them and the children can copy them.

2   **Asking a child to lead *Switch***
Some children respond well to the responsibility of leading *Switch*.
The leader, of course, becomes the composer as well as a
performer. If you have led *Switch* a few times with the group,
leaders will probably understand that you expect them to produce
patterns which others can copy, and that each pattern should be
sustained for some time. But just occasionally you may need to
intervene when a child leads with the intention of catching people
out. Usually, your main role will be supportive; attentive copying
by you helps leaders to clarify and remember their patterns.
Having a child lead *Switch* is of value to all the children present –

16

not just to the one who is leading. It helps to dispel any notion that music is something that teachers lead and children follow.

3 **Changing the rules**

Try playing *Switch Two*. This starts like *Switch*, with the leader repeating a pattern and the children copying. After a while, you move on to pattern two, but the children stay on pattern one. When you say 'Switch', the children move to pattern two. After the children have repeated pattern two for a while, you move to pattern three, with the children joining you after you say 'Switch', and so on. Children are likely to find *Switch Two* much harder than *Switch*. Start by choosing very easy patterns such as repeated, even clapping, or repeated, even slapping, until the children have mastered the idea of the overlap. In *Switch Two*, children learn to recognise a new pattern whilst sustaining an old one, and become less dependent on the leader. Thus they are developing their performing skills, increasing their own responsibility for the accuracy of their performance and, probably, becoming more observant of the performance of other children.

Conductor

Like *Switch*, *Conductor* can be played by full classes, or smaller groups. Again, it is suitable for a wide age range, though young children are probably best introduced to it in a small group. As in *Switch*, it is best to introduce *Conductor* by leading it yourself. Sit the children in a circle, and stand in the centre. Ask each child to think of a sound she or he can make, and then hear them one at a time, making suggestions to any child who has not thought of a sound (e.g. 'Clap, or say "Ah"'). Once a sound has been heard, each child is expected to stick to his or her own sound until a new leader is chosen. Next, explain the game like this: 'I am a conductor, and you are my orchestra. When I point to you, start making your sound. Carry on, until I show you that I want you to stop.' After checking that the children understand your signs for starting and stopping, compose a piece by directing children to start and stop playing as you wish. Again, do not issue any verbal instructions. If you want a child to play louder, softer, or differently, you must show them with an appropriate signal. Children then take it in turns to conduct the orchestra.

Again, we will evaluate this activity by considering the musical process, and the opportunities for musical assessment and general assessment (see pages 11–12).

In *Conductor*, as in *Switch*, the leader is composing, the group is performing, and everybody, one hopes, is listening. But the nature of the composing and performing that are taking place is different. *Switch* always results in a piece based on short repeating patterns. *Conductor* can result in pieces with no observable rhythmic structure.[2] *Switch* results in a composition that is linear or – in the case of *Switch Two* – has two overlapping strands. In *Conductor*, pieces can have as many layers as there are children. From observing children whilst they are members of the orchestra, a teacher can see their level of concentration, and ability to control their performance according to the conductor's instructions. Watching children conduct gives insights into their development as composers.

I once played *Conductor* with a class of 9-year-olds whom I had not met previously. We were using percussion instruments, not body sounds. After leading the game myself once, I asked for volunteers. I was not impressed by the compositions produced by the first three conductors. They were high-spirited boys who enjoyed the power of leading the game, but did not seem to spend much time listening to the results of their instructions. They were acting as though they were on point duty, rather than being in charge of an orchestra. Their compositions consisted of a succession of very loud sections which were so short that we never had a chance to get used to them before they changed. These children were not used to being given this sort of responsibility and they were acting as though they might never be given it again. When a fourth boy volunteered, I noticed some of the other children nudging each other. Robert was an immature child who could hardly read or write. The other children seemed to think that he would be a hopeless leader. Nothing could have been further from the truth. With great assurance, Robert pointed to a triangle, and listened to it being played for a full ten seconds before directing the player to stop. He turned to a tambourine and listened to it for a similar length of time before directing that player, also, to stop. He turned to the triangle again, and when it had played for a few seconds, brought the tambourine in on top of it. He listened to the two sounds together for a while, and directed the tambourine to play a little louder to achieve the balance he wanted. His piece continued with the same care. Robert used silence as well as sound. Finally, after three or four minutes, Robert brought his piece to a gentle, but purposeful, conclusion. When he sat down, there was a short silence, and then the children, quite spontaneously, applauded. Robert had shown us all a lot about his musicianship. He had also made everyone present start to listen closely to the sounds they, and everyone else, were producing. He had earned the respect of his peers, and done wonders for his own self-esteem.

Neither *Switch* nor *Conductor* requires teachers to have musical skills more advanced than those of the children they are leading. Indeed, leading *Switch*, and certainly *Switch Two*, is easier than playing it. The teacher manages the activities through teaching skill, not musical skill.

Traditional games

Many adults recall playing singing games and clapping games as children. *London Bridge is Falling Down* and a clapping game, *A Sailor Went to Sea*, are two that I remember from my own primary school playground. In former times, singing games were a diversion for adults as well as children. Today, they have moved firmly into child culture. Children, mainly girls, organise them for themselves in some school playgrounds. And adults lead some with young girls and boys at home, in playgroups, and in the earliest stages of the infant school. Can these games form part of primary music? Let us consider one in particular: *Ring a Ring o' Roses*.

Ring a Ring o' Roses

This singing game is found in a multitude of versions. However, it is generally agreed that this is the first verse:

> **Ring a ring o' roses,**
> **A pocket full of posies.**
> **A-tishoo! A-tishoo!**
> **We all fall down.**

Usually, everyone skips in a ring until the end of the verse, when they fall on the floor.

This is an old singing game, though quite how old is not known. The original meaning of the words is uncertain. One story – which is probably not true – is that the game dates from the Great Plague of 1665, with the four lines of the verse denoting, respectively, the plague rash, herbs carried as protection against infection, the sneezes of the dying, and their demise. Iona and Peter Opie (1985: 221), who collected and researched children's traditional games over many years, attribute the supposed association, perhaps a little cynically, to

'. . . satisfaction of the adult requirement that anything seemingly innocent should have a hidden meaning of exceptional unpleasantness'. They found no reference to the game being played in England earlier than the mid-nineteenth century.

Suppose that a small group of 5-year-olds are playing *Ring a Ring o' Roses*, led by their teacher. In what musical processes are the children participating? And what can the teacher learn from their response? This is a performing and listening game. The children are singing a song, and combining it with some physical actions which may be in time with the music. They may not sing the song perfectly in tune, but are having the sort of practice which does, with most children, result in them progressively learning to sing better in tune. They are listening, because they sing the song at roughly the same pace as everyone else. As in *Switch*, they may also be guided by looking, particularly at the moment when they should fall down.

The teacher learns about the children's singing ability and their rhythmic awareness. Some children may always sing below the pitch that she chooses but move up and down at roughly the correct points. Others may use a very limited range of notes, or even only one note. A few may not have found their singing voice: they may be speaking. This is information that the teacher can use to help children develop their singing in the future. Some children may be anticipating the moment when they fall down, thus demonstrating that they know the song, and are able to think ahead.

The range of traditional singing games and clapping games is considerable. In *The Singing Game*, Iona and Peter Opie (1985) list over 150 such games, many of which come in several versions. Some, such as *Ring a Ring o' Roses*, *Oranges and Lemons*, and *London Bridge is Falling Down*, are well known, and appear in many children's songbooks. But singing games are being invented, and changed, by children all the time. Teachers can learn a lot about children from just watching them playing games in the playground. And that is surely not musically threatening to anyone.

As well as traditional singing and clapping games, there are some other well-known music games which are sometimes played at children's parties. *Musical Chairs* and *Musical Statues* are two examples. Children move round while music plays. When it stops, they either race to sit on a chair (of which there are too few available) or become still as a statue, as appropriate. These are competitive games usually played when there is an adult available to adjudicate on matters such as who got to the chair first, or whether Samantha moved or not. Too much competition in school music is not a good thing. But these games are not completely devoid of musical value. They may help children to learn to move in time to music, for once one child does this, others often copy. And children have to listen, not just treat the music as background. Otherwise, they will soon be out.

Music games with borrowed structures

Most games can, with a little imagination, be turned into music games. Take *Hunt the Thimble*, for instance. Instead of saying 'getting warmer', or 'getting colder', as a child hunts the thimble that was hidden whilst she was out of the room, children can be asked to sing a note which gets louder as the hunter gets closer. This challenges the hunter as a listener, and the rest as performers; it is not easy to control the loudness of sung notes, particularly long notes. There are many possible variations of this game. Sung notes could get higher as the hunter approaches the thimble. Or clapping could get faster, for instance.

Bingo can be played using instrument sounds instead of numbers. The bingo cards might show pictures of the instruments, which would be played out of view. During *Musical Snakes and Ladders*, for instance, there could be special sounds for going up ladders and down snakes, and, perhaps, some musical tasks to perform if particular squares are landed on. Figure 1 (p. 22) shows a composing board game which I have called *Coach Trip*. As in an ordinary board game, the object is to get from the start to the finish using a sequence of dice throws. In this case, the game re-creates a school trip from Oxford to Stratford. Whilst dice throwing is taking place, the players sing songs they sang on the coach. When a counter lands on a square with instructions, the players, as a group, compose a suitable piece.[3] The teacher is free to invent his or her own rules about matters such as whether the final square must be reached by an exact throw, how the instructions for compositions should be interpreted, and whether there is one team, or rival teams. Board games may follow the line of a story, perhaps *Jack and the Beanstalk*. They may take children on real or fantastic journeys, or in quest of buried treasure. The possibilities are almost limitless.

But games are only one way of facilitating composition. In the next chapter we turn to some other approaches.

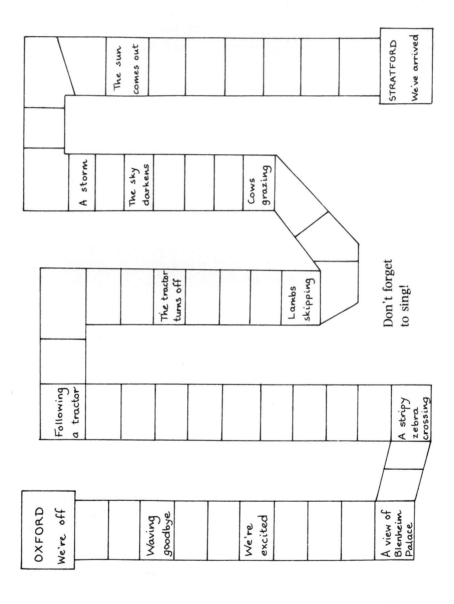

Figure 1 *Coach Trip*, a board game for some Oxford children who have recently returned from a school trip to Stratford.

Composing

'The material of music is sound and silence. Integrating these is composing.'

John Cage in *Silence* (Cage, 1968: 62)

What is composing?

Composing is not just about producing string quartets that Mozart might have written if he had lived longer, or writing substantial orchestral works for first performance at the Henry Wood promenade concerts. Composing takes place whenever a person (or group of people) devises a piece of music. It may be a ten-day opera cycle based on *The Complete Works of Shakespeare*, or a one-minute setting of a haiku. It may use the resources of a full symphony orchestra, or three chime bars.

I shall use the term *composing* to encompass all acts of musical invention by anyone in any style. Thus I take activities such as improvising or arranging to be particular styles of composing – not distinct processes.[1] I shall describe the people composing – be they adults or children, highly qualified or inexperienced – as composers, and the pieces of music they produce as compositions. In this, I am observing the conventions of other arts areas. We speak of children and adults as writing and being writers, whether their output – their writing – is an account of yesterday's visit to the zoo, a daily diary entry, or a novel shortlisted for the Booker Prize. We speak of children and adults as painters whether they paint their paintings in a classroom, at evening class, or in a garret.

Composing in school

Visit any primary school, and you are likely to observe children making art: painting, writing poems, and so on. But you may not

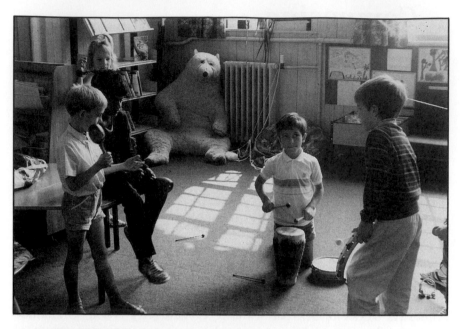

Group composing. The boys here are working together, and not as individuals.

observe anyone composing. Why is this? The simplest answer is that music in school traditionally has stressed performing and listening at the expense of composing. Primary teachers rarely composed when they were at school. Those who studied music after they left school trained, typically, as performers, not composers. This is changing. The amount of composing going on in primary and secondary schools has been increasing for some time. About a third of the marks in GCSE Music (DES, 1985c) are allocated to composing. Composing is part of the National Curriculum (DFE 1995, Welsh Office 1995) for all children from the age of five years. Many students entering initial teacher training already accept composing as an integral part of music making. But for several decades to come there will still be primary teachers whose experience of children composing is secondhand. These teachers can, quite understandably, feel some uncertainty about how to approach composing with children.

Many opportunities for composing arise naturally as part of classroom activity. A child who has written a poem may offer to make it into a song. A group of children who have improvised a drama about a haunted house may want to include music to set a spooky atmosphere. Here, the teacher's job is to encourage the children – to facilitate their development of their own idea – and to respond to their work when it is complete. But we cannot rely on children's ideas alone for a programme

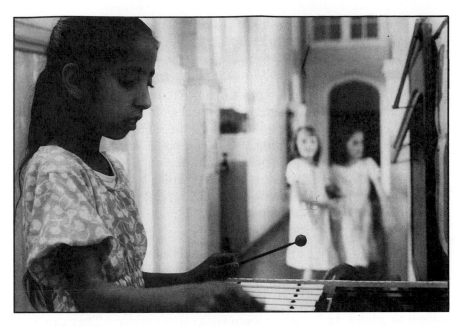

Individual composing. Nadia has been composing alone on the glockenspiel, with great concentration, for more than half an hour.

of composing. We need to promote situations in which children wish to compose, provide input to enrich their composing, and respond to their work so as to help them learn from it.

I shall focus on approaches to composing that are collaborative, involving children working together as a class or in smaller groups. I do this for two reasons. First, group composition is easier to manage. It demands fewer resources, and requires the teacher to be in fewer places at once. A class of thirty children in small groups requires fewer reasonably quiet working spaces than the same number of individuals would need. Second, group composition offers more opportunity for learning. For most people, composing is not about sitting in front of a blank wad of music manuscript paper and waiting for the muse to provide inspiration, but a form of problem solving. John Paynter (Salaman, 1988: 29) speaks of his own composing as '. . . setting up problems for oneself, taking decisions that will answer those problems, and having the satisfaction of having answered them.' Composing in groups can enhance the processes of selection and rejection inherent in problem solving. Group composing is not a hybrid procedure designed by music educators – a sort of *educational composing.* It takes place in the world outside school too. Much – though not all – jazz, for instance, is collaborative composition. However, children will of course sometimes prefer to compose on their own.

Getting started

How can a teacher introduce children to composing? Ideally, they introduce themselves to it. Young children are fascinated by sounds of all sorts: rustling paper and birdsong, as well as the sounds of singing and musical instruments. Extensive opportunity to play with sounds can lead, without deliberate adult help, to the sequencing of a series of sounds to give a result that pleases the composer. This process is often seen, or rather heard, in children who make up songs from an early age.[2] And children who have a piano, or other instruments, in their homes often love to experiment on them. But many children arrive at school without this sort of experience.

From their earliest days in school, children can play with sound. This can be organised by means of a music corner, or a music table, in which children can play on their own, or in small groups. A music corner can contain many types of sound makers, not just official musical instruments. Children can be encouraged to bring interesting sounds to school, and to share them with other children. They can find a variety of sounds from the same sound maker, thus developing their association between physical action and the nature of sound. They can learn to listen closely to sounds, to talk about them, and compare them.

What about the noise? Certainly, there will be some. But teachers can learn to manage it. In the past, primary classrooms were often very quiet places, in which children spoke only to their teacher. Today, teachers tolerate a higher working noise level because they accept that children learn from talking to each other too. Like talk, music cannot take place in silence. And music tables are often distracting only whilst they are novel. Teachers who have introduced them often speak of ceasing to notice them by the end of a fortnight or so. This is not because the music table receives progressively less use, but because the teacher has learnt to regard the resulting sound as ambient noise. Particularly whilst music tables are being introduced, teachers can help themselves by including only fairly quiet sound makers. There is no need for the first instrument placed on the music table to be a large cymbal.

Children who grow up with music tables in their infant schools often start to compose of their own accord. Teachers can receive frequent requests to 'come and listen to what we've made up'. But one can sometimes meet a junior class, even an upper junior class, who have not been encouraged to play with sound in the past. In this situation, a more systematic approach to starting composing may be needed. A general instruction to the children to 'go and compose something' is unlikely to be productive; children who have not played with sound makers do not know what sounds are available to them, and cannot control them. Some initial familiarisation with materials, and the sounds they produce, is necessary.

A vast range of materials is available for composing: the voice and other body sounds, classroom percussion instruments, the piano and orchestral instruments, recorders, improvised instruments, and so on. Initially, we will focus here on classroom percussion instruments. Most schools have at least a modest collection, and they are the first real instruments that many children meet. Children of all ages can use them, often alongside other materials. And they can provide a way into music making for musically deprived older children who are unlikely to be impressed by suggestions that they experiment with sounds produced by odds and ends, and who may be embarrassed at the thought of using their voices in an improvisatory way.

Materials 1: Classroom percussion instruments

One sometimes hears, and reads, the statement that classroom instruments come in two categories: pitched and unpitched. This is misleading. The so-called unpitched instruments – woodblocks, cymbals, triangles, and so on – have sounds that include an element of pitch. Most people will agree that a triangle sounds higher than a woodblock, and that a small triangle sounds higher than a large one. Take a good-quality cymbal, and notice how the pitch of the sound changes as you hit it in different places, or with different beaters. The main way in which these instruments differ from the so-called pitched ones – glockenspiels, metallophones, xylophones,[3] chime bars, and so on – is that their pitches are not tuned to correspond to the notes found on the piano. It is more precise to speak of the two categories as tuned and untuned instruments.

Classroom instruments are expensive items. Many are also fragile. Matters concerning care which seem obvious to us can be less clear to young children. Many percussion instruments are played by being hit, an activity not often encouraged at school. If it is all right to hit some instruments, why not try hitting all of them? When we predict that we are likely to break a maraca if we hit it with the stick we have just used on a drum, we are drawing on many years of experience of hitting various objects and observing the results. When we hold a maraca, our experience of materials and their mass enables us to predict that the bulbous end is a thin, hollow, shell. Indeed, we may have seen a broken maraca, and so know that the shell is brittle. Similarly, when we predict that a triangle beater is likely to scratch, or even perforate, the head of a drum, we are drawing on experience of scratching which we would prefer children not to acquire on the school's expensive instruments.

Whatever care is taken, instruments will occasionally be broken. The size of the school music budget needs to reflect the limited life of instruments. And we cannot expect children to be creative with instruments if they are worried about breaking them. But children can learn to regard instruments as special, and to think before they act. Careful introduction of instruments helps with this, and also serves the musical purpose of encouraging children to observe closely, and learn to control, instrument sounds.

Instruments can be introduced one at a time, when the whole class is together. Try passing an instrument round the class, and encouraging experiment and talk. What different sounds does the instrument make? How can we describe the sounds? How is the instrument made, and how should we look after it? What is the instrument called? Are any of the sounds like those produced from other instruments? The following might form an extract from an introduction to a single maraca:

— How is Katy playing the maraca? . . . . . .
— Yes, by flicking her wrist . . . . . .
— How can you describe the sound she is making? . . . . . .
— Katy, now play the maraca like Richard was doing, using more of your arm . . . . . .
— How is the sound different?

Throughout the exercise, the emphasis is on listening, often very fine listening. Try not to give the impression that there is a single, official, way of playing any instrument, but encourage range and variety of sound, permitting any means of playing the instrument which cannot damage either it or the children. Once a range of sounds has been produced, several of the children have handled the instrument, and you are sure that points concerning care have been understood, the instrument can be placed on the music table, and children will do their own experimenting as the occasion arises. Later, you can share what the children have found. Gradually, other instruments could be introduced in a similar way. As new instruments are added to the music table, others may be removed temporarily. There is no need for children to have continual access to all instruments. Working with just a few resources from time to time can help to focus activity.

Why do I consider that official ways of playing instruments should not be stressed at this stage? I think that prescription of technique can constrain listening and thinking, and so impede musical development. I remember my introduction to the triangle, when I was about 6. My teacher said something like this:

> 'This is a triangle. See how I am holding it, so that the triangle hangs from the piece of string. Watch how I hit it . . . . . . Now I'll hold the triangle while you hit it . . . . . . Now try holding the triangle too.'

After a while, I did learn to hit the triangle without it twisting round on its string. But I cannot remember the sound it made – only the physical difficulty of producing it at the correct time. There was a sense in which the class percussion band became PE, not music, for me. And it was many years before I even thought of trying to find other ways of producing sounds from a triangle.

As I recall it, my infant class included at least fifty children, and I am amazed that my teacher managed to give me any individual attention. I understand why, in this context, letting me experiment on a triangle before joining the percussion band would have seemed a pointless and noisy waste of time. But now, with more manageable class sizes, experiment is feasible. Of course there are times when I want a child to produce a neat *ting-ting* from a triangle to give a particular effect. On these occasions I will, if necessary, direct the child to hold the instrument in a particular way. But, during composing, and many performing, activities, children can be left to choose the sound that they think is most effective. If they want the damped sound obtained when a triangle is held firmly in one hand, and hit close by, so be it.

So far I have focused on the effect of physical action on sound. If we perform a particular physical action, what sort of sound do we get? This is only one side of the relationship between sound and action. When we hear a sound, can we work out how it was made? Can we go to an instrument and repeat it? There are many ways of building up this association. Games can be useful. Two groups of children can be given equivalent sets of instruments and seated on either side of a screen. A member of one group plays a sound. The other group confer and then echo the sound. The teacher and the rest of the class are able to see both

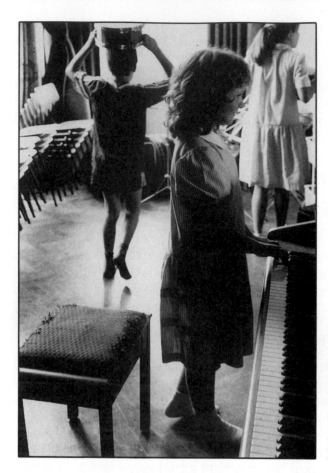

Alice is practising some of the less conventional piano sounds she has chosen to contribute to a class composition. She prefers to stand up so that she can see other members of her group, and reach the extremes of the keyboard with both hands.

groups, and learn from finding out which sounds the children confuse. This is a taxing game; two or three contrasting instruments will be sufficient to begin with.

Materials 2: Other resources

There are many other materials for composing. The instruments that children bring with them – their bodies – are a valuable resource. Vocal sounds, including singing, and other sounds such as clapping and stamping can add greatly to the range of sounds available. They need not be a last resort to be used when there are not enough percussion instruments; they are more suitable than instruments for some purposes. On page 40 there is a report of a composition for which

Steven and Gareth play
electronic keyboards and
amplify their vocal
sounds, alongside David,
who has chosen to play
the bongos in this class
composition.

some children elected to use mainly vocal sounds, despite there being
a large range of instruments available.

Children learning portable instruments, such as the violin or the
recorder, can be invited to bring them to composing lessons. Composing
strengthens the association between action and sound, and so also
helps with performing. Instruments that belong to individual children
are probably best played only by them because of the possibility of
breakage. But a piano, if available, can be a useful resource for any
child, not just those taking piano lessons. Like all instruments, it can be
played in unconventional, as well as conventional, ways.

Recent developments in technology mean that electronic keyboards are now available in many primary classrooms. Often, they can
be integrated with other available materials. An increasing number of

primary schools are obtaining music software for computers. Some of it effectively converts the computer into a musical instrument which can be played alongside others. With other software, it is more appropriate for the children to compose using the computer alone.

Instruments may be improvised. Coconut shells are a permanent part of many instrument collections. Later, on page 41, we shall see how items including vacuum cleaners may be used occasionally for particular effects. Children who find objects which make interesting sounds may wish to use them in composing activities.

Improvised instruments can be used to enrich the sounds available from a collection of classroom percussion instruments, but they cannot be substitutes. Given the cost of good classroom percussion instruments, it can be tempting to stock the percussion trolley with home-made ones. Unfortunately, many physically outlive their period of musical use. A yoghurt pot containing gravel does not sound as interesting as a maraca. Once its maker has forgotten the excitement of assembling it, it is best disposed of. A yoghurt pot can be a very boring instrument to play. And when you become bored, you stop listening, and playing degenerates to become mere mechanical action.

Planning composing: The need for experiment

Children who have not played instruments for a while forget the sounds they make, and lose their control of them. Consequently, it is often expedient to start a composing lesson with an opportunity for experiment on the instruments available. Let us suppose that you have decided to take a full class composing lesson using classroom percussion instruments as your only sound materials. You have a class of thirty juniors, and thirty-five instruments available. How will you organise the experimentation?

You have a number of decisions to make. Will you allow the children to choose their own instrument? Will you offer them any guidance about their style of experimentation? How will you terminate the experiment? In general, I prefer to allow children to choose their own instrument, to permit them some unstructured experiment, and to end it through use of a pre-arranged signal, such as three taps on a drum.

Some teachers worry that children will start to behave badly if they are given percussion instruments. In fact, the high spirits which do sometimes arise are often the result of over-enthusiasm, rather than naughtiness. The children want to play the instruments, and they become impatient if a lot of time is spent on administration. This tendency towards over-enthusiasm is particularly strong amongst children who are rarely allowed to play instruments. In the words of an advisory teacher: 'If you are nine, and you have never played a drum before, and you think you might never play one again, you will give it a jolly good bash while you have the chance.' So when working with a new class, I always explain, right at the beginning, that:

○ nobody is to play except when I say so
○ this is so that we do not waste any of the time we could be using for playing.

Also, I waste as little time as possible by arranging the room so that instruments can be chosen and collected speedily. I find an arrangement in which the children are seated in a circle, and the instruments are on the floor in the middle, particularly efficient. You may have other ideas.

Once I have started the experiment with some statement such as 'see what different sounds you can produce from your instrument', I move among the children listening to what they are doing. When I decide that they have done enough experiment – perhaps after a minute – I give the pre-arranged signal and everyone, usually, stops. There is no need to have a particularly loud signal. The point is that the children nearest you will stop immediately, and the rest soon follow them. After the experiment, I might ask some children to demonstrate their sounds, and make links into the composing we are going to do if possible.

Sometimes, you will find a class surprisingly quiet during experiment. Later, you may wish to encourage them to find some loud sounds too. More often, classes will make plenty of noise. This is particularly likely if they have had infrequent access to instruments in the past. Problems of perpetual loud playing usually resolve themselves as children come to realise that they will meet the instruments again. You can accelerate this through musical ploys such as asking children to find quiet sounds as well as loud sounds. But it would be unmusical to ask children to 'experiment quietly'. Music is sometimes loud, and children need access to loud music as well as to quiet music, without feeling that they are being naughty.

33

A composing lesson

Composing often takes place as a small group activity. But what might a composing lesson for a full class look like? Clearly, it could take many forms. Here is a single example of a lesson that is intended to introduce a class to composing. It is an account of a lesson I taught to a Year 4 class. Once the National Curriculum in music is well established, it is likely that composing lessons for this age group will need to be more demanding. The lesson is written up in such a way as to bring out some points that I want to make about planning, implementing, and evaluating composing activities. However, teachers find their own ways of recording teaching, and the format I use here is intended as an example only, and not as a model.

Lesson plan: Introduction to composing

GROUP   Class of twenty-nine children aged 8/9

DURATION   Approximately forty minutes

LOCATION   School hall

AIMS
(for lesson)
- To introduce the children to group composing
- To reinforce the children's understanding of the concept of duration (long/short) in musical sound
- To introduce the children to symbolic notation

OBJECTIVES
(for children)
- To listen closely to the sounds that classroom instruments produce
- To find ways of producing sounds from instruments, particularly sounds of differing duration
- To use symbols to differentiate short sounds from long sounds
- To compose pieces that draw on resources of short and long sounds, and to notate these compositions symbolically
- To evaluate these compositions

MATERIALS   About forty classroom percussion instruments
Paper and pens

METHOD
1. Children choose instruments. Demonstrate the signal for stopping playing (clapping hands four times).
2. Children experiment to find three different sounds from their

34

instruments. Listen to some of the sounds. Draw out the idea that some sounds are longer than others.

3   Children experiment to find the longest and shortest sounds that their instrument can produce. Listen to some pairs of sounds. How might sounds on particular instruments be made even longer or shorter? Are there some instruments that can make only fine differences between long and short? Listen carefully to a very long sound produced by a sustaining instrument, e.g. finger cymbals. Do we all think that it has died away at the same time?

4   Show my notation for a long sound followed by a short sound (see Figure 2a on page 37). Can the children work out what it represents? Ask them to play it as a class. When I tell them to start, I want them to play their longest sound. When that has finished, they are to play their shortest sound. The piece ends when the last short sound has finished.

5   Ask for suggestions for a slightly longer piece. Play it according to the same rules as Figure 2a.

6   Ask for suggestions about a different way of playing the new piece. If there are no ideas, suggest that we synchronise the start of each sound by having a child playing a sustaining instrument directing us. Record us playing the piece that way, and play the cassette back to the children. What do they think of it? How might we improve it? Or if everyone thinks it is wonderful, why do we like it so much?

7   Divide the class into five friendship groups, and give each group a sheet of paper and pen. Ask each group to make up a piece using the ideas of long and short. Each group should notate its composition. They can use the system of notation provided, or invent their own. Disperse the groups around the room. Check that groups are working profitably, but avoid the temptation to give them ideas unless they are stuck.

8   After about ten minutes, or earlier if everyone has finished, give the signal for children to stop playing. Ask each group to perform their piece and show their notation. Ask for comments from the composers and the audience on the pieces and the notation.

9   Discuss ways of taking these suggestions into account in future compositions.

REPORT (The numbers here correspond to the numbering of the method.)

1   The children were excited by the prospect of playing the instruments, but showed commendable self-control. The signal worked

well. The children nearest me stopped immediately, and everyone stopped within five seconds.

2   The children enjoyed doing this. I chose some examples of children playing conventionally, and less conventionally, for us to listen to, and tried not to give the impression that I was valuing some techniques more than others. The concept of long/short arose naturally from talking about two sounds which Julie had produced with the finger cymbals: tapping one with the other to produce a long sound, and bringing them together to produce a short sound.

3   The children quickly spotted that they had very little control over the duration of some instruments, e.g. maracas. Robert's long maraca sound involved a longer arm movement, but very little difference in duration. We listened to the sounds with our eyes shut to confirm this. While we were listening to Julie's long finger cymbal sound, some children furthest away from her noticed the whir of the fluorescent light. We discussed how the sound is always there when the light is switched on, but that we only notice it when we are listening very carefully.

4   This was straightforward.

5   Tony suggested the notation given as Figure 2b.

6   Tony suggested that we synchronise our sounds, and I asked Julie to lead us from the finger cymbals. When we listened to the recording, Robert said that it sounded boring because the cassette recorder had failed to pick up the quiet sounds at the end of the long sound. Hannah suggested that a long sound be deemed complete after a count of ten.

7   I moved round the groups as they worked, but they had plenty of their own ideas.

8   All groups used my system of notation. Four groups wrote longer linear combinations of dots and dashes. Two groups synchronised their sounds, and the other two expected individual players to be guided by their own instrument. The fifth group wrote two independent parts: one for *long* instruments that sustained well, and the other for *short* instruments that did not. There were more sounds in the part for short instruments (see Figure 2c). The first four groups were impressed by the fifth group's idea. Comments about the other compositions were polite and general, e.g. 'It was good'. There were no analytical comments, and no composers said anything about their own piece.

9   We discussed how we might make a longer piece using long and short sounds. The general consensus was that it would be

36

interesting to develop further the idea of separate parts for long and short instruments.

COMMENT
We came some way towards accomplishing all the objectives. However, the children's evaluation, both of their own and other children's composing, was limited. The most productive evaluation was of the recording. In future lessons, perhaps I should make more use of recording, but also encourage constructive criticism of our own, and each other's, work.

FUTURE WORK
Short term   In the next lesson, we will work on producing a longer piece using long and short sounds.

Long term   I do not want the children to get stuck in a long/short rut. We will try other sorts of stimuli, and other approaches to notation including, of course, not using it at all.

The general points about composing lessons that I wish to draw out of this account are as follows:

1   **Use of stimulus**
The stimulus here was 'long and short'. I chose it as a musical concept well within the reach of most Year 4 children. But stimuli

Figure 2   Three long/short compositions. The third (c) has a separate part for *short* instruments which do not sustain well.

37

do not need to be musical concepts, and they can be used in a variety of ways.

2   **Choice of materials**
Classroom percussion instruments provide a variety of long and short sounds. But I would have welcomed any suggestion from the children that body sounds be included.

3   **Response to composition**
There was time for reflection, discussion and criticism, though this was not a particularly successful feature of the lesson.

4   **Appropriate use of notation**
I chose a form of notation that reinforced the long/short concept. There is no value in using notation for its own sake.

5   **Facilities**
The lesson suited the available facilities: a hall in which several groups would be able to work without distracting each other.

The remainder of this chapter develops these points.

Stimulus

Stimuli for composing can take many forms, including poems, objects, pictures, stories, words, pieces of music and musical concepts. They are used to give composers starting-points for their ideas. An effective stimulus helps composers, particularly those working in groups, to spend less time deciding what to do, and more time deciding how to do it. Stimuli can be chosen by teachers or composers. Indeed, a composer may think of one spontaneously. For instance, a child who has written a poem may, without any suggestion from a teacher, wish to set it to music.

An intended stimulus can become a constraint. Teachers need to intervene if no worthwhile work is being generated. Equally, they will sometimes wish to allow children who have deviated from the stimulus, but who are working productively, to see their ideas through.

Some stimuli can be interpreted more divergently than others. There are some occasions when teachers wish to allow children considerable freedom. At other times, perhaps when teaching a musical concept, teachers may wish to define the parameters for the composing more closely. Thus, in the long term, teachers often use a combination of types and levels of stimuli.

Earlier, on page 34, I gave an example of a lesson plan based on the stimulus of a musical concept. Below, I use accounts of composing activities to illustrate some ways in which other types of stimuli may be applied. They are only examples; you will have your own ideas.

Stimulus 1: A poem written by a teacher

A class of Year 5 children were to be introduced to composing through their topic: *The Sea*. Their teacher wrote the following poem to remind her class of some images associated with the sea:

The Sea

Waves lap gently on the seashore
Fishes dart
Black clouds bring a raging storm
Out peeps the sun and shines upon a rainbow
Waves lap gently on the seashore

Sally Crowther

The teacher organised this poem carefully. Each line is short, and easily remembered. The contrasting first four lines suggest different styles of music. Repetition of the first line as the last line implies repetition of the first musical idea, thus enabling the children to realise that they can repeat parts of their music.

After reading and discussing the poem with the children, the teacher read it one line at a time, inviting the children to improvise suitable music at the end of each line. Individuals produced different effects for each line. Lee, for instance, who was playing a xylophone, interpreted the poem as follows:

Waves lap gently on the seashore	Slow upward glides over six or seven notes.
Fishes dart	Fast upward glides over ten or eleven notes. Gaps between glides.
Black clouds bring a raging storm	Loud rapid succession of single notes using hands alternately.

39

Out peeps the sun and shines upon a rainbow	Gentle, slow, succession of upward and downward glides, interspersed with isolated notes.
Waves lap gently on the seashore	As before, with a few downward glides.

But the combined effect of twenty-seven children performing as individuals was that each line sounded much the same as the rest. As the children were concentrating on what they were doing, and apparently unaware of the overall effect, the teacher played them a recording of their performance, and invited comments. Stuart described it as 'rubbish'. Gradually, the children started to analyse the problems with the recorded piece: 'It sounds all the same'; 'It is too crowded'. In John Cage's terms, quoted at the start of this chapter, they had failed to integrate silence with sound. Silence seemed not to have been considered at all. John Cage's advice to a young composer of a 'busy' over-written score that 'there is not enough of nothing in it' would again have been appropriate. The class had concentrated on sound, and neglected silence. Suggestions about how the piece could be improved were made. Some children thought that there should be fewer performers. Others thought that some instruments were unsuited to particular lines, or that individuals were playing them in an inappropriate manner. The class rehearsed each of the lines again with children only joining in when they thought their instruments suitable. The children thought that this was an improvement, but had many ideas for further development. The sea music developed into a project to which the children returned at intervals over the next six weeks. By the end of this time, children were divided into four groups, one for each of the four different lines. Each group had developed their piece over several weeks, refined their choice of instruments, and, finally, notated the music so as to show its organisation. Figure 3 is a copy of the graphic score drawn by the *Fishes dart* group.

Stimulus 2: A published story

A term later, the same class had been listening to extracts from the *Narnia Chronicles* by C.S. Lewis. They decided to compose a piece entitled *The Creation of Narnia*. Initially, groups of children worked on segments of the story, and drew graphic scores which they stuck together in sequence. In other words, they started by organising their

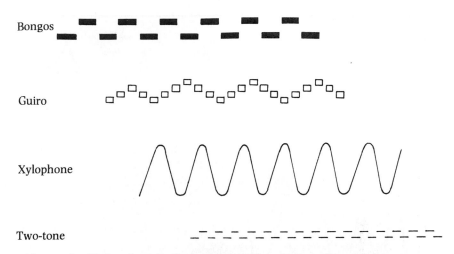

Figure 3   *Fishes dart.* Each instrument has its own line, and a
symbol which reflects the performer's perception of the
shape of the single sound chosen. The four parts are
staggered to show a progressive start and finish. The
horizontal scale is not literal; there were many more
sounds than are shown.

composition like the finished version of the sea music. This time they
were not satisfied; they wanted a continuous piece, not a series of
chunks. At the children's request, and with their guidance, the teacher
copied the individual scores onto a long sheet of paper, linking each
group's work through the modification of beginnings and endings of
sections. The class then determined the interpretation of the new score,
drawing on the experience of the individual groups. The teacher co-
ordinated the performance by moving a ruler along the score, which
was more than 15 metres long (see extract, Figure 4). At the start of the
project, the children used classroom percussion instruments. Later they
found it easier to achieve some of the effects they wanted with their
voices. The final piece was almost entirely vocal.

Stimulus 3: A collection of instruments chosen by a teacher

At the end of the school year, the same class devised some
'machine music' to be included in a performance of John Paynter's
Space Dragon of Galatar.[4] The teacher offered a stimulus of three
machines – a banda machine, a photocopier and a vacuum cleaner.
The class listened to these, and then collected more machine sounds

Figure 4   An extract from *The Creation of Narnia.*

using improvised instruments such as rulers, abacuses and rough paper which could be scrumpled and torn into shreds. Next the children discussed how to organise their piece so that even the quietest sounds could be heard. Eventually, the sounds were arranged according to their loudness, and introduced progressively with the quietest sound first. The piece ended when the teacher gave a signal for all the instruments to gradually wind down.

Stimulus 4: A child's painting

Paul, aged 6, had painted a picture of himself standing outside his house. The sun was shining and the sky was blue. His teacher asked how he was feeling in the picture, and Paul said he was very happy. Would he like to make some 'happy' music to go with the picture? Paul chose a xylophone. He focused on five adjacent notes, choosing a dance-like rhythm. He finished with a glide along the whole length of the xylophone, moving from the bottom to the top. His teacher said that she had enjoyed his 'happy' music. Would he like to play some 'sad' music now? No he would not. He was feeling very happy.

Stimulus 5: An object chosen by a child

Jane, aged 7, brought a seashell into school. Her friends passed it round, and observed it closely. They described it as cold, smooth, and curly. They made some cold, smooth and curly sounds and assembled them into a piece of music.

Stimulus 6: A verbal description

A class of Year 6 children had been working within a topic of *Pets*. They decided to make up a piece about a particular dog who had visited the class the previous day. Their teacher collected a list of words which described the dog: four-legged, brown, hairy, warm, barking, and so on. Next, she asked for suggestions of sounds to represent the words. 'Four-legged' was easy enough. Anna chose a drum and hit it four times. But what would the children make of 'brown'? Darren volunteered to find a 'brown' sound. He chose a xylophone and tentatively played a few high notes. 'That's not brown, it's green,' said Sean. Sean then played a few quiet, slow, low notes on the xylophone, and all the children, including Darren, agreed that it was a superior 'brown' sound. The class continued through the list. Eventually, they had twelve sounds. Children took turns to play them whilst another child constructed a piece about the dog by conducting them, as in the *Conductor* game described in chapter 2.

Stimulus 7: A piece of music chosen by a child

Katy, aged 9, had worked out how to play *Twinkle, Twinkle, Little Star* on an electronic keyboard, starting on the note C. She had taught it to her friend, Sarah, and they were playing it together with Sarah starting on the highest C available, and Katy two Cs lower down. Their teacher suggested that Katy should work out another part to play, whilst Sarah played the tune. Katy started by playing her first note – the low C – all the way through. Eventually, she produced a slow-moving part based round low C, but with occasional, careful, use of the adjacent B and D.

Stimulus 8: A piece of music chosen by a teacher

A class of Year 2 children were working within the topic of *Colour*. Their teacher played them an extract from each of the movements of Bliss's *Colour Symphony* (1922) naming them, as Bliss had done,

'Purple', 'Red', 'Blue' and 'Green' respectively. The class then devised some 'Black Music' which they contrasted with some 'White Music'.

With the exception of *Twinkle, Twinkle*, the composing activities described above all involve the transformation of experience in some medium other than sound into music. In some cases, for instance the machines and the storm, there has also been transformation of sound into music. It is not always easy to transform experience in sound into music. One can end up just copying the sounds closely to produce sound effects, not music. This can result in an exceedingly disjointed product, particularly when poems or stories are involved. For example,

'He ran down the corridor'
(*Sounds of someone running down a corridor*)

'He slammed the door'
(*Sound of door being slammed*), etc.

This sort of work can be a first stage of production of a composition, but it has not got there yet. Although the ability to copy sounds is useful, and shows fine listening and performing ability, it is not, on its own, composing. Composing is about transformation, not translation. A piece of music is not judged by the extent to which it is an accurate copy of something else, but as a piece of art in its own right. There is room in music for sound effects. But they need to be used as part of the music, not as a replacement for it. An example of this is found in *The Creation of Narnia* (see page 40). The score for the section on the creation of animals (see page 42) illustrates the use which the children made of impressions of animal sounds. But the jagged line running through this section represents a musical idea – a rising and falling melodic pattern sung to 'Ah' – which was present through most of the piece. The animal sounds were part of the development of this idea. In other words, they contributed to the musical development within the piece.

Some established composers have also used sound effects to enhance a musical idea. The cuckoo effect in Delius's *On Hearing the First Cuckoo in Spring* is one example. Here, the effect is realistic enough for us to recognise that it depicts a cuckoo song. But the context in which it is set is impressionistic. It is not intended as an accurate copy of the sound and silence which typically accompany cuckoo song. It is a different quality of experience.

Pop music, too, uses sound effects. One example which children may be able to locate in their family record collection – possibly next to Dad's old flared jeans – is The Move's *Fire Brigade* (1968). Vocal impressions of a (now superseded) fire engine siren in the chorus complement an introduction by an apparently genuine fire engine. But the whole effect is nothing like that of a real fire engine racing to deal with an emergency. There is none of the panic, or danger, or relief that it is not your house on fire. The whole piece is, I think, a well-organised, and skilfully timed, joke.

Much music is free of association with any named stimulus: a story, a poem, lyrics, or a visual image. Think, for instance, of all the untitled sonatas and symphonies. Children can compose without an external stimulus too. When children spontaneously make up pieces at the music table, this is often what they are doing. They are not always depicting *Winter*, or telling the story of *Goldilocks and the Three Bears*; they are stringing sounds together for the joy of it, or rather the sound of it. Often, however, an adult asks the composer what the piece is about, and the child supplies a title to please the adult.

Stimuli are useful devices for facilitating composing. Established composers, as well as children, use them from time to time. But we need to avoid the idea that music can be composed only in response to a stimulus, that it has to be about something or other. If we are not careful about the ways in which we use stimuli, children can lose the ability to work with sound for sound's sake. They can come to regard composing as a sort of reversible system for transmitting secret messages. The composer takes the stimulus, and disguises it as a piece of music. The audience takes the piece of music, and guesses what the stimulus is. Seems a bit pointless, doesn't it?

Choice of materials

Earlier in this chapter (pages 27 and 30), we considered some uses of a range of materials: classroom percussion instruments, orchestral instruments, body sounds, and improvised instruments, for instance. A teacher's choice of materials depends on a number of factors: availability, suitability to the composing task in hand, children's experience, and so on. Often there is no point in restricting the materials available. But there are occasions when a teacher has a particular reason for offering the children a selection. Perhaps the teacher feels that a class that has become preoccupied with rhythm at the expense of melody would benefit from a period of working only on tuned instruments.

45

Should a teacher restrict the sounds that a child makes with a given instrument? Again, not for the sake of it. We have already considered this issue with reference to instrument technique (see pages 28–29). It arises also in the context of the selection of notes available to players of tuned instruments.

Children are sometimes introduced to composing by playing tuned instruments with some of the notes removed. In particular, one will see children restricted to the notes C D E G A, or even just a subset of these notes. This five-note (pentatonic[5]) scale occurs in many musical contexts such as Hungarian folk song, Scottish song, and other styles of folk music. It forms the basis of two classic approaches to music teaching: Carl Orff's *Schulwerk*, and Zoltan Kodály's *Choral Concept*, both of which draw on pentatonic folk song. Used in such an authentic, or at least integrated, context, or even to produce a special effect, pentatonic composition can be worth while. However, children are sometimes restricted to this pentatonic scale for another reason: no combination of notes drawn only from this scale sounds violently dissonant to Western ears.[6] I find this an unfortunate approach. First, children do not need to listen to what they are doing: everything will sound all right. Second, children are unable to reproduce some music they know; they cannot, for instance, play the melody of *Twinkle, Twinkle, Little Star*, or many pop songs. Third, children do not get a chance to play with dissonance and make their own decisions about whether to include it in their compositions. Children can be given all the notes in the Western (chromatic) scale – the black and white piano notes – for many composing activities. And when they are using instruments, such as string instruments, which can produce other intervals as well, why not let them explore non-Western scales and the notes between semitones as well?

Responding to composing

Your response helps children to evaluate their work, and learn from it. It also helps you to understand what the children have achieved and learnt, and to decide what activity might be appropriate next. It is rarely appropriate just to thank children for their piece and move on.

The accounts of composing activities described earlier in this chapter give some examples of response to composition. Response takes three main forms: questioning, suggesting, and encouraging.

Questioning helps you to find out more about the composing process than you observed whilst the children were working:

o Why did the children start the piece that way?
o Did they reject any ideas?
o If so, on what grounds?

Questioning also helps the children to evaluate their work:

o Are they pleased with it?
o Why?
o Are there any parts which they think could be even better?
o How might they improve them?
o Are there any differences of opinion within the group?

Teachers can be reluctant to make *suggestions* for two reasons. First, there is the view that as composing is a creative activity, all the ideas should come from the children. Of course we must value children's ideas. But this does not mean that we should never tell them some of our own. We are employed to teach, not to observe, and teaching includes helping children to benefit from some of our more relevant ideas. In any case, much questioning is actually suggestion in disguise. For instance, the question, 'Do you think your piece of music is too short?' is asked typically by teachers who think that the piece *is* too short, and have ideas about how they would lengthen it, given the chance. Suggestion has its place; we just need to recognise when we are making suggestions, and when the children are working things out for themselves.

Second, teachers may be reluctant to make suggestions in response to composition through concern that what they say may not be sensible. This is a particular worry for teachers who feel they are not familiar with the vocabulary that accomplished musicians use when talking about music. A suggestion given in plain English is not necessarily any poorer; it may well be superior, and is certainly more likely to be understood by the children. When you hear a piece of children's composition, you will usually think spontaneously of suggestions you could make. It can be helpful to draw parallels with an art form about which you do feel more confident to make suggestions. My initial thoughts about compositions are often similar to those about stories. Have the children worked out how to start? Have they worked out how to stop? These questions are not so simplistic as they sound. Young children often begin playing when you ask them to, and carry on until you ask them to stop. Having thought about the beginning and

47

the end, what about the bit that comes in between? Is it going somewhere, or are the ideas disjointed, and not developed? Are there too many, or too few, ideas? Is the end a logical conclusion, a well-organised surprise, or a disappointment, as in a story which suddenly ends with 'and then we woke up and realised it was a dream' or 'and then we went home for tea'?

Other children can be drawn into discussion of composition. They often have pertinent points to make, and helpful suggestions to offer. They learn as composers from constructive criticism of the work of others. The composers may have set a poem by using different music for each line, with the result that the piece is a series of disparate chunks. How can that be resolved? Ask the children (see page 136). Open discussion means that children's compositions can be compared, and it helps with listening too: 'What pattern did you play, Mark?' 'Did anyone else have a pattern like that, alternating between two notes with the same letter name?' 'Let's listen to Mark's group again, and check that we can hear his pattern'.

The third aspect of response is that of *encouraging*. There are times when questioning and suggesting are inappropriate: the children are doing very well on their own, and you just wish to encourage them to carry on.

We respond to children's composing partly because of our wish to see their work as part of a progressive music education. When listening to their work, we are always alert to ways in which we could promote progression. But this progression will not necessarily be accomplished through further revision of the same piece. Mozart did not continually revise the symphony he wrote at the age of 8. He did the best he could with it at that particular time and moved on, showing his progression through the music he wrote later. Sometimes, the most appropriate teacher response to a composition is simply the suggestion that the piece is now complete, followed by the offer of another stimulus intended to help the children progress.

Questioning and suggesting make more sense if children can remember their composition. It is useful to record compositions onto cassette as a matter of course. Recordings need to be made quickly and efficiently. The better the equipment, the more useful the recording will be. But a functional recording can often be made with a suitably sited ghetto-blaster with a built-in microphone. As well as assisting with immediate response to composing, recordings can be used as a record of children's achievements in music, and are a valuable resource when a teacher, or children, wish to reflect on progress made in music.

One final point about response to music. Music has its own meaning, not all of which can be expressed in words. When we talk about music, we comment only on parts of it. The whole is more than the sum of the parts. Thus a verbal description of a piece is never more than a pale copy of the original. Talking about music is valuable because it enables us to communicate some of our ideas. But it is never a substitute for the experience of music itself.

Notation

Notation is simply a means of recording a composition. There are many composing activities in which notation is not necessary because the composition is recorded in another way, for example it is remembered or stored on a cassette. The machine music described on page 41 was such a case.

Where we do wish to use notation, it needs to be of an appropriate form. In my long/short lesson (see page 34), I chose a form of notation that reinforced the concept we were exploring. Staff notation, for instance, would have been inappropriate because we were not playing rhythms which could be notated conveniently by symbols such as crotchets and quavers.

The links between music and visual symbol are interesting and ambiguous; notation, like words, can never account for more than some aspects of music. But the relationship between music and symbol, like that between music and talk, can be exploited in the development of composing. The use of sound pictures, such as those given in Figure 5, can help with the establishment of this relationship.

Sound pictures can be used to structure experimentation. Adults would probably have little difficulty thinking of a way of representing the first picture (Figure 5a) on a tuned percussion instrument. Most would use a single beater to glide from the bottom to the top of the instrument and back down again, three times. For the second picture (Figure 5b), many would choose a single pitch and either just play it once (if it sustained well), or repeatedly (if it did not). They would see the third picture (Figure 5c) as a combination of the first two, and deal with it accordingly. The fourth picture (Figure 5d) might provoke them to think about, and revise, the speed of the glides they made for the first and third picture. Replace the fourth picture with exactly the same shape drawn in red instead of black, and they would probably laugh politely. Colour is irrelevant, isn't it? They probably would not like the

49

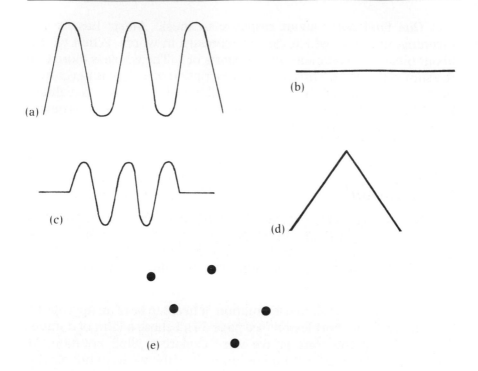

Figure 5 Sound pictures.

fifth picture (Figure 5e) much. It cannot be accommodated within the system they have developed in which the picture is read from left to right as a graph of pitch against time.

Children, particularly young children who have not learnt to read music, often do not make these assumptions. They may choose to read from left to right, or from top to bottom, or may read the whole picture, or each shape, as a unit. They may vary loudness instead of pitch, or they may just draw the shape with their beater as they play up and down, seemingly at random. As in the piece about the dog (see page 43) they may not have learnt that colour is irrelevant. (Is it?) Children's responses to the fifth picture are diverse.

We learn from this that there are many possible relationships between music and symbol. We may wish to make sure that children learn our adult relationship; this will eventually help them with staff notation which does read from left to right, and is, in a sense, a graph of pitch against time. But perhaps we can preserve the other relationships too. This is not because they are childish, but because the adult system is arbitrary. Other systems offer opportunities for different sorts of music. And as we observe the relationships that children establish between sound and symbol, there is much that we, as composers and teachers, can learn.

Facilities for music

As music consists of sound, it has particular requirements for facilities. Having several groups of composers within a classroom can create so much volume that it becomes difficult for children to hear the results of their own work. In fact, children seem much better able to cope with the competing noises than their teachers. This is probably because children are interested mainly in their own piece, whereas teachers have learnt to notice what is going on throughout the classroom.

Teachers can develop their tolerance. But alternative arrangements, also, can help. One solution is to use a larger room, such as the hall, if available. A second is to use more than one work area. For instance, you might arrange for a group to work in a cloakroom. Naturally, the feasibility of this suggestion depends on the arrangements for the supervision of children within your school. Third, you may prefer groups to compose in turn whilst the rest of the class are doing something else; perhaps art or mathematics. This arrangement can offer further advantages over the whole class composing at the same time. First, all groups have access to the entire pool of available instruments. Second, groups can work at their own pace; they do not all have to finish together. Third, compositions can be performed to the class individually. This can improve the quality of discussion considerably. With the best will in the world, it is very difficult for children to concentrate on a series of four or five performances, particularly if they are excited about their own.

Noise through the walls is another consideration. Some schools seem to have been designed without thought to the fact that music makes a noise, and yet requires quiet. In schools where music is valued, everyone accepts that they will overhear other classes making music from time to time. Naturally, there is give and take. Teachers need to know that there will be times of each day when they will not be disturbed by music. But this is not just a matter of music only taking place when neighbouring teachers have given their permission or are out. It really is give and take. A teacher at a junior school where music is thriving explains: 'Of course there are quiet times. But if a teacher in the classroom next door is doing a creative music lesson, you would not plan to do silent reading.'

In schools where music is not so well established, teachers may, initially, be less tolerant of the sounds of composing in the next room. One problem is that the combined sound of several groups composing can seem chaotic to a teacher on the other side of a wall. Indeed, it can sound as though the children are just messing around. Teachers convinced that children are working become more tolerant. Try inviting teachers into your room to *see* what is happening. Alternatively, take composing lessons in a room such as the hall which other teachers walk through. Include examples of children's composition at times of sharing, perhaps during assembly.

Early in my teaching career I took a composing lesson with a class of 11-year-olds. Each group was working purposefully and enthusiastically from a workcard, and I was really pleased with how things were going. Four groups were using classroom and orchestral percussion, and the fifth was using the inside and outside of the piano. In the next room was an experienced and very kind craft teacher mindful of the disruptive behaviour which probationary teachers can sometimes face. Clearly, he thought that I needed his assistance, for he came into my teaching room with his cane. As he strode into the room, his face wore a firm, even fierce, expression. As he looked around him and saw the children sitting on their chairs, discussing their ideas, and trying them out on instruments, his expression changed to one of utter surprise. From his side of the wall, it had not occurred to him that the children were working. From my side, there was no doubt of it.

Performing

'. . . how can we expect to produce a vital performance if we don't re-create the work every time? Every year the leaves of the trees reappear with the spring, but they are different every time.'

Pablo Casals in *Conversations with Casals*
(Corredor, 1956: 196)

This chapter focuses on activities in which children are interpreting music which is already composed. Thus we are at the second stage of the sequence

composing → performing → listening.

Performing, like composing, is a creative process. The musician's frame of reference is different, for the composition is already there. But, to paraphrase Pablo Casals' statement, no two performances of the same piece are, or should be, identical.

Performers receive instructions from a composer, which they transform into music. But however these instructions are given – verbally, or through graphic or staff notation perhaps – they do not say all that there is to be said about the piece. An interpretation of a Chopin *Prelude*, for instance, in which the pianist just played the notes written and only got louder, softer, faster or slower in response to the composer's markings, would be dull, and not what Chopin wanted. In a sense, performers flesh out the bare bones of pieces devised by composers. Often, when performing, musicians focus on accurate interpretation of the composer's instructions. Accuracy is important. But it is not the be-all and end-all of performing. There is nothing slavish about performance. It can be every bit as exciting as composing.

In school, performing can take place on voices, instruments, or a combination of the two. I start with singing, and later add some instruments. I do not assume that teachers are able to accompany themselves on the piano, guitar, or any other instrument. Teachers who can do this will have no difficulty working out how to apply their skill in those songs and instrumental pieces which benefit from accompaniment.

Starting singing with children

Primary teachers vary in their confidence as singers. Some sing seemingly without a care in the world, regardless of the situation. But many are self-conscious about singing from time to time, or even all the time. There is nothing new about this. In 1597, Thomas Morley opened one of the earliest known music theory textbooks, *A Plaine and Easie Introduction to Practicalle Musicke*, with a self-styled non-singer's account of an embarrassing incident:

> . . . supper being ended, and Musicke books, according to the custome being brought to the table: the mistresse of the house presented me with a part, earnestly requesting me to sing. But when after manie excuses, I protested unfainedly that I could not: everie one began to wonder. Yea, some whispered to others, demanding how I was brought up . . .
>
> Morley, 1952: 9

What did Philomathes, the speaker, do about this? Give up going out to supper? Claim to have perpetual laryngitis? No. The extract continues:

> . . . upon shame of mine ignorance, I go nowe to seeke out mine olde frinde, master Gnorimus, to make my selfe his scholler.

In other words, Philomathes determined to conquer what he perceived as a problem. Clearly, this fictional incident was set up by Morley. If Philomathes had not decided to take lessons, then there would not have been much point in Morley writing his book. But there is a serious point to it. Singing can be developed. Many, possibly all, of those who claim to be unable to sing, or to sing with any confidence, can improve their ability. And although it is more straightforward to learn to sing as a child, it is possible at any age. There are plenty of examples of student teachers learning to sing confidently during teacher training, or teachers learning after several decades in the profession. One cannot learn to sing overnight, but, with sustained practice, it is possible.

Philomathes was not worried only about singing. The reference to the 'Musicke books' suggests that his concerns included singing unfamiliar melodies from notation: sight-singing, as it is sometimes called. No one is born able to sight-sing. It is a skill which must be learnt, and is usually taught. Ideally, practice in sight-singing starts in youth, but there are plenty of adults who learn it. I doubt that sight-singing is beyond the reach of any teacher. However, a great deal of singing with children can take place without it. Sight-singers' only real advantage over everyone else is that they are able to learn new songs more quickly.

When planning singing with children, you can take your own initial confidence into account. You can organise singing so that you are faced only with challenges that you feel ready to meet. That way, your confidence will grow. And, as we shall see, there is no need for children to lose out when you organise their singing in such a way as to develop your own confidence.

Teachers often start singing with a new group of children by teaching them a song. Whilst this can work very well, it can be highly stressful for the teacher. It involves an element of leaping into the unknown. Will the children like the song I have chosen? Will they know it already? Will it be too difficult for them? Will I be able to teach it to them? We rarely operate like this in other areas of the curriculum. Usually, we find out what children are able to do, and plan accordingly. So consider starting singing with children by singing songs they already know. You will need to know them too. Ideally, learn them by sitting in when the children are singing with someone else. In any case, practise them before leading the children yourself.

If children are to make a confident start to a song, then they need to know what note to start on, and when to begin singing. How will they get this information? A sung starting note is easier to copy than one played on an instrument, and is customarily given by the teacher. This can be the aspect of the singing lesson which is most intimidating to less confident singers. How will I know what note to sing? What if the note wobbles? In fact, you will probably find that if you know the song really well you will come out with a sensible note. Listen to the start of the song in your head before you sing it, and your starting note is more likely to be secure. But if you do not feel ready to sing a starting note alone yet, there are alternatives. Before the lesson, find a suitable starting note on an instrument such as a glockenspiel. When the time comes to sing the song, play the starting note. If you feel up to singing it, do so. If you do not, ask the children to sing it, and join in, singing something like 'this is your starting note'. You will probably find that you only need to do this as a temporary measure, but even if you need to

55

use a glockenspiel every time, the children will not suffer; they will be learning to take a note from an instrument.

There are many ways of actually starting the singing. Perhaps the easiest is to set the beat by clapping, and then, clearly, take a breath in time to start singing. If the children are watching you they will breathe with you and you will start together. Again, you will set an appropriate speed if you listen to part of the song in your head before you start. If all this sounds too much for you to begin with, just start singing, and the children will soon join in.

Singing with children like this helps you to find out about the children's experience as singers, and means that your planning of future singing can be more effective. It helps you to become accustomed to singing *with* children before you need to sing *to* them. And it helps children to become accustomed to your voice. Children unused to singing with broken voices, for instance, will adapt much easier if they are singing a song they know.

One of the most important keys to successful singing with children is preparation. Nobody can successfully lead a song that they do not know properly, or they have not worked out how to start, or how to finish, or how to organise. Accomplished music teachers can seem to manage without preparation. In fact they are just displaying techniques which they have rehearsed to the point that they appear automatic.

Choosing songs

How might we go about selecting songs for children? A song is a combination of lyrics and music. It can be helpful to start by considering these two dimensions separately.

When choosing a poem or story to read to children, thought about language level is second nature. If we want children to notice the words of songs, and to develop their language through singing, then we need to be just as selective about lyrics. It is common, however, to find complex language in the songs that children sing. *The Miller of Dee*, a song included in radio broadcasts for schools on several occasions up to at least the mid-1980s, provides an example. It is a setting of Isaac Bickerstaffe's poem *There Was A Jolly Miller*.[1] The first verse is as follows:

There was a jolly miller once lived on the river Dee,
He danced and sung from morn to night, no lark so blithe as he;
And this the burden of his song forever used to be:
'I care for nobody, no, not I, if nobody cares for me.'

Were we to read this poem to children, we would, at least, talk through the meaning of some of this language. 'No lark so blithe as he' is not trivial. 'The burden of his song' has provoked some articulate adults to consult their dictionaries. In singing this song with children, we would, also, need to explain the meaning of these expressions. If this does not seem worth it, then it might be best to choose another song. The only nonsense songs children sing should be those written as such. Otherwise, there is a danger that children will switch off from the words altogether, and so miss out on an important dimension of the song.

Next, I turn to the music of songs. Children develop their singing through being challenged, but they need to be presented with material that is largely within their capabilities if they are to make any progress. This is just a special case of the general principle of matching the task to the child. The complexity of describing the melodic difficulty of songs is illustrated in the work of two Argentinian researchers, Silvia Malbran and Silvia Furno (1987), who used eighteen variables of pitch, rhythm, structure and expression to draw up profiles of some 400 songs. We shall briefly consider just two musical aspects of songs: their melodic range, and their melodic shape, or contour.

Children have a small vocal range which is, generally, relatively low. Graham Welch (1979) reports reference to this in a *Musical Times* article of 1890, but adds: '. . . the practice of fitting children's voices to the published repertoire, rather than the other way round, is still prevalent . . .' (Welch, 1979: 25). Images of choristers singing high melodies with enormous range seem to have masked the fact that children, left to their own devices, sing lower. This is illustrated by a comment of Iona and Peter Opie (1985: vi), the singing-game collectors referred to in chapter 2, that 'children seem inclined to choose a rather lower pitch than might be expected – sometimes a little too low for comfort.' Even these experienced observers of children's song seemed to view children's choice of low pitch as deviance which needed to be justified, rather than evidence of a preferred low range. Children learn to sing in tune by singing in their comfortable range, and develop a wider vocal range by gradually extending it. So it is important that much singing takes place in this range. Vocal range is an important

57

issue when we come to consider the development of children's singing. I raise it at this stage as reassurance to the considerable number of women teachers concerned that their singing voice is lower than the children's. Women teachers who think they have low singing voices usually find that their comfortable range is similar to that of children. Men teachers usually find that children are comfortable singing in a range an octave above them.[2] Sing songs at a pitch you find comfortable, and the children will probably be delighted.

Some melodies are much more awkward to sing than others. In general, melodies that leap around are harder than those that consist mainly of stepwise motion. This is partly because large leaps tend to take the melody out of the comfortable range, but also because they require considerable vocal control. The easiest way of assessing the difficulty of a particular melodic contour is to sing it yourself. And if you choose songs that you find straightforward, children will find it easy to follow you.

Another consideration when choosing songs is that of variety of content, musical form, and musical style. There are times – such as Christmas, or during work within particular topics – when it can be appropriate to sing a series of similar songs. And a teacher's repertoire of songs is likely to be stronger in some areas than others. But in the long term, variety in song is as beneficial as variety in reading matter and so forth.

In *Music from 5 to 16* (DES, 1985a: 3), HMI suggest that the infant curriculum should include opportunities to sing songs in the following categories:

- o alphabetical, counting, sorting, cumulative songs
- o nursery and folk songs
- o singing games
- o religious songs, some of which can be used in school assemblies
- o modern, 'pop', and 'fun' songs.

Clearly, this list implies variety in form, content and style. As infants will often rely on their memories for recall, many suitable songs are very short. Nevertheless, the forms suggested are not confined to single short verses; repetition is used to generate songs with choruses, and songs which grow each verse (cumulative songs). Children who sing songs from all these categories will be singing for a variety of purposes: to reinforce language and mathematical concepts; during play and assembly; and as part of an explicitly musical experience. They will be learning traditional songs and adult songs, as well as those specially composed for schoolchildren.

HMI's list for junior children is also wide-ranging:

- o   traditional folk songs and ballads
- o   songs from other lands and other cultures
- o   songs from former times
- o   modern songs including some 'pop'
- o   songs for all seasons
- o   songs for assembly
- o   simple descants, ostinati and second parts in conjunction with the above
- o   rounds and canons
- o   music in and for drama.

DES, 1985a: 6

As far as content and style is concerned, the most significant addition is that of songs from other cultures. However, there is no reason why variety of culture could not also be represented in infant song, particularly, perhaps, in classes that include children from contrasting cultural backgrounds. Junior children are able to tackle longer songs. In addition, the list suggests various second-part forms including descants,[3] ostinati,[4] rounds and canons.[5] Second parts are usually added progressively to some songs that children know well; they are not typically taught initially.

Teaching songs

There are many musical and efficient ways of teaching any song. When deciding how you will teach a song you have chosen, you will have in mind your knowledge of the children: their enjoyment of singing, likely concentration, and so on. There are two other factors to be considered:

- o   the structure of the song
- o   your previous experience.

Two aspects of the structure of a song may influence your choice of teaching method: its length, and the use of repetition. Long songs need to be subdivided in some way, or the children will be unable to remember them. Repetition within songs – for example a chorus – can be exploited to make learning more musical and efficient. If the children learn the repeating elements first, they become aware of the pattern within the song, and are able to sing substantial parts of it early in the learning process. Taking length and repetition into account, there are three main ways of organising the learning of a song:

1 **Absorption**
   The song is repeated until the children know it. This can be an effective way of teaching very short songs.

2 **Segmentation**
   The song is divided into sections, for example lines, which are taught one at a time, usually in the order in which they appear in the song. The first verse of a song might be taught in this way.

3 **Segmentation + absorption**
   This is a combination of the two processes. Part of the song is taught through segmentation, and then the remainder is absorbed. With a song of several verses and a chorus, the chorus might be taught first, line by line. Then the teacher might sing the whole song, inviting the children to join in with the chorus. By the time that the end of the song is reached, the children may know the melody of the verse too. Teaching the children the words to some of the verses might be left to a later occasion; it is far better for children to know only one verse and be eager to sing all of them, than to half know all of them, and never want to hear the song again.

Ideally, lyrics are memorised during the learning process. Once children know them, they can concentrate on singing unhampered by reading. But this is not always feasible with long songs. A single large word sheet, or perhaps an overhead projection, is often preferable to many individual copies. Having the children look upwards, and in the same direction, can lead to better singing posture, and a greater sense of ensemble. For many songs, it is not necessary to write out all the words. A few key phrases or pictures can be enough to jog children's memory. Actions can also help with recall of words.

How might your previous experience affect how you teach a song? You will want to choose a procedure with which you feel you can cope. Below, I suggest a general procedure for teaching songs. At each of the three stages, I suggest options for those who do not feel confident to tackle the approach suggested. Implementing these options does not necessarily decrease the musical experience of the children. Their most significant disadvantage is that they require greater preparation, and so make less efficient use of teacher time. So there is something to be said for gradually learning to operate without some of the options, at least for some songs.

Stage 1   The teacher sings the song to the children

This is so that the children know what they will be learning. Particularly when the song is to be taught through segmentation, this can increase motivation. It can be difficult for the teacher to appreciate the need for preliminary performance because he or she already knows the song.

OPTIONS
o   Teach the song to a small group of confident singers in advance. Use them to support your singing.
o   Arrange for another teacher, or a child, to provide a supportive accompaniment to your singing.
o   Use an accompaniment on a pre-recorded cassette.
o   Sing along with a pre-recorded cassette that includes the song as well as the accompaniment.

Stage 2   The teacher teaches the song to the children

Organise this through absorption, segmentation, or a combination of the two, according to the structure of the song.

OPTIONS
o   As for any of the Stage 1 options.
o   Use a pre-recorded cassette that systematically teaches the song. This may be purchased, or provided by another teacher.

Stage 3   Everyone performs the song

This gives the children a sense that they have achieved something. With a long song, performances will be necessary at several points during the learning process.

OPTIONS
o   Use the support of a supplementary accompaniment, or a pre-recorded cassette, as suggested for Stages 1 and 2.

Try to teach songs as a continuous piece of music, not as a series of disjointed phrases. This is particularly important if you decide to teach a song line by line. If you give clear instructions in advance, it is possible to go through a whole verse without stopping, or even interrupting the beat, as follows:

You sing line 1. Without a break, the children echo it.
Without a break, you sing line 2, and the children echo it.
And so on.

Consider the following alternative method of organising line-by-line learning:

You tell the children that you are going to sing line 1.
You sing line 1.
You ask the children to echo line 1 after you have given a signal.
You give the signal, and the children echo line 1.
You tell the children that you are going to sing line 2.
You sing line 2.
And so on.

The only advantage of the second method is that it requires less initial organisation by the teacher. On the other hand, it has the following disadvantages:

- It takes longer, and so is potentially more boring.
- The children do not find out how the lines fit together.
- The children have a greater opportunity to forget each line before echoing it.
- The beat is disrupted, with the effect that the feeling of participating in a continuous piece of music is lost.
- More complex signals are needed. In the first method, you can just point to yourself, or the children, when necessary and supply eye contact as appropriate. In the second method, you will need to provide a rhythmic signal, and also to sing starting notes for individual lines.

Teach words and notes together when you can. After all, you know both the words and the notes, and if you sing a verse to *lah*, or whatever, you probably still have the words going through your mind to help you. Eventually, you may find that some sequences of words or notes are so difficult that they need to be practised on their own. But by this stage, the children also will know how the words and notes fit together.

62

As soon as you think the children will be capable of getting through the song, or its first verse, let them have a go at it. Some problems may iron themselves out when you put the lines together, and segmented teaching mangles language in a manner that is best sustained for as short a time as possible. Whatever mistakes arise during the run-through, try to let the children continue for at least a few lines. Unnecessary stopping and starting disjoints the music, and some mistakes will correct themselves without the need for verbal instructions from you. Here, male teachers are at an advantage. As they sing an octave lower than the children, the correct model is always audible, even when some children are in error. Women's voices tend to get mixed up with the children's.

Above all, singing should be fun. Do not feel that you have to carry on singing a song until everyone is singing it perfectly. That time may never come. You can always try to smooth out some rough corners or teach another verse on another occasion. It is far better to have the children wanting to sing for longer, and eager to sing in the future, than to have them bored.

Developing singing

Singing must be enjoyable. If it is not purposeful, it soon becomes tedious. There are many respects in which children's singing can be developed: tone, control, vocal range, volume, expressive quality, and so on. Here we focus on developing one aspect of children's singing that has implications for all the others: the ability to sing in tune.

Many children have difficulty singing in tune. Quite how many depends, of course, on how you measure this. But Arnold Bentley (1968), in a substantial questionnaire survey of British schools, found that roughly 25% of 7-year-old boys and 11% of 7-year-old girls were reported by their teachers to lack 'co-incidence at the unison'. By the age of 12, the figures for boys and girls had reduced to about 7% and 1% respectively. Bentley's investigation illustrates two patterns which have emerged in a range of studies. First, at any age, more boys than girls have difficulty pitching their voices. Quite why this is the case is not known. The difference in figures is too great to be accounted for solely by boys' so-called 'developmental lag'; gender stereotyping is probably a contributory factor. Second, as children get older many learn to sing in tune. In other words, there are many schoolchildren for whom the problem seems to resolve itself. But can we help children to develop accurate pitching earlier? And can we do anything to help the substantial minority of children, particularly boys, who remain unable to sing in tune?

Children's ability to sing in tune often depends on what they are singing. In particular, much depends on whether the song lies within their comfortable vocal range. Try singing a song which is too high or too low for you. What happens to your tuning? As stated earlier, most children have a vocal range that is small and low. With practice, this range can gradually be extended. But whilst we are teaching children to sing in tune, it makes sense to choose songs that lie within their range. What might this range be? This is likely to depend on the previous experience of the children. Listen to children singing in the playground and notice the range they use. Cleall (1970) found that infant boys were most comfortable in an octave range of G to G across middle C. Infant girls preferred a slightly higher and wider range: just over an octave from A to B. Many modern children's songbooks include songs in a suitable narrow, low, range.

How can you organise singing so that good pitch singing is developed? Clearly, it is not possible to devise a recipe that will work in all situations. But the following three principles may be helpful. First, children need frequent opportunities to sing. Singing need not be confined to singing lessons or even to songs: try singing the register, for instance. Second, singing needs to be organised as an activity which everyone participates in without a sense of embarrassment; each individual contribution, no matter how out of tune, is valued. Finally, children's individual progress in singing must be monitored. This is impossible if singing is organised only as an activity for large groups, for example two or more classes. Massed singing from time to time can be a marvellous social and musical experience. But, on its own, it is unlikely to do much to develop the vocal accuracy of those children who need special help. There just is no time to identify individual need, let alone respond to it.

How can we help children who still do not learn to sing in tune? There are three straightforward things we can do. First, we can check that the low range in which we are singing is comfortable for these children. Ask a child to sing a note of her or his choice, and see if it falls within the range. If it does not – and it is more likely to be below the range you are using – sing in this child's range some of the time. Second, we can ensure that the poor pitch singers are not all bunched together, unable to hear anyone who is in tune. This is not just a bit of social engineering, but a way of helping them with their singing. You may have had the experience of finding your singing becoming more relaxed and more accurate when you are next to a good singer, partly through resonance. Third, if children are aware of their difficulty, we can encourage them to think about it with optimism. Rather than saying something like 'Never mind, we can't all be good at everything, and you are good at running', we can point out that children develop at different rates in all sorts of ways – for instance some are taller than others – and that their singing will develop as they get older. In the meantime, they need to be given many opportunities to sing. Nobody ever learnt to sing in tune by not singing at all.

Vocal accuracy, though important, is only one aspect of singing. Nobody – teacher, parent, or child – should become obsessed with it. It is untrue that anyone who cannot sing in tune is necessarily 'unmusical' – whatever that means. An accurate singer demonstrates fine pitch hearing; an inaccurate singer may have just as fine hearing, but have poor control of the vocal mechanism. So the use of the term 'tone deaf' to describe someone who sings out of tune is inaccurate. A few years ago, I met Andrew, a 6-year-old who had been rejected from a neighbourhood choir because of his poor pitching. According to his score on my Pitch Test (Mills, 1988a), his ability to observe the difference between pairs of notes which were very close in pitch was unusually high. Indeed, it exceeded that of all the 250 other 6- to 8-year-olds whom I tested. Clearly, Andrew was not tone deaf. In fact he was an unusually determined little boy. He wanted to get into that choir, and his parents had overheard him trying to teach himself to sing in tune by matching his voice with piano notes. By the time he was 9, he was reported to be singing in tune, and to be a promising trumpeter. But not all children have Andrew's persistence or opportunity. It is important that we do not write off developing singers as unmusical.

Last, a brief word about the development of two other related aspects of singing: breathing and volume. Children's breathing during singing can be guided from the earliest stages of development. Breathing at the ends of phrases produces a melodic flow which makes pitching easier, and, of course, preserves the meaning of the lyrics. As children learn to control their breathing, they become more able to sing long phrases without a break. But it is possible to place so much emphasis on the technicalities of breathing that singing becomes more aligned with PE than music. In the earliest stages of singing, it can be sufficient for the teacher to set a model of breathing at sensible points, and to draw the children's attention to this.

Concerning volume, it is not uncommon to overhear children being harangued for not singing loud enough. Yet when they try to sing louder, they can end up just shouting. Young children's voices are, by nature, quiet. Apparent volume can be increased by encouraging children to look up. Actual volume develops with age, but can be accelerated by good posture – an upright seated or standing position – and attention to breathing.

Writing songs for children

The Runaway Seed

The runaway seed fell into the ground and it grew, it grew,
The runaway seed fell into the ground and it grew, it grew.
The runaway seed fell into the ground
Off the tree with a leap and a bound
And it grew, grew, grew, grew, grew.

A little white shoot looked up at the sun and it grew, it grew,
A little white shoot looked up at the sun and it grew, it grew.
A little white shoot looked up at the sun
So now the tree had really begun
And it grew, grew, grew, grew, grew.

The rain came down and watered the tree and it grew, it grew,
The rain came down and watered the tree and it grew, it grew.
The rain came down and watered the tree
Then it was bigger than you and me
And it grew, grew, grew, grew, grew.

The ginormous tree reached up to the sky and it grew, it grew,
The ginormous tree reached up to the sky and it grew, it grew.
The ginormous tree reached up to the sky
Its branches stretched from side to side
And it grew, grew, grew, grew, *GREW.*

Sally Crane

The Runaway Seed, as you probably became aware as you read it through, is an alternative set of lyrics for the song *The Runaway Train.*[6] Sally Crane wrote these words following a fruitless search through songbooks for a song which tied in with some work on seed growth which she was leading with Year 3 children.

There are many situations in which there is no song to fit our purpose. We can spend ages hunting through the indexes of songbooks to no avail. All the songs on our subject are slightly off the point, or the range is enormous, or the language is archaic. Writing our own song is a real alternative. And, of course, songwriting does not need to be left to those occasions when no suitable song is available.

As we have seen, songwriting need not start from scratch. You can write lyrics to fit a melody you know, or a melody to fit a suitable poem. Children can be involved, or even do all the songwriting. They often make up their own words to songs, so why not make the most of their enthusiasm? There are many feasible approaches. Sally Crane started by singing through *The Runaway Train* and letting the words take shape. This meant that the words developed in a pattern which suited the melody. *The Runaway Seed* is not the greatest poem since Wordsworth, but the fit of the words and music is excellent, and the children were thrilled that it had been written especially for them.

When making up a song, just let your ear be your guide. If you like the melody and it is easy to sing, and the words seem to fit well, it is likely to be successful.

Voices and instruments

Many songs are effective on their own; others sound more complete with the addition of some form of instrumental accompaniment. This can take many forms according to the nature of the song, the musical expertise of the teacher and children, and the availability of instruments. Often, the most effective accompaniments are very simple: complicated ones quickly swamp the song. Judge by ear whether or not an accompaniment is suitable.

Infants and juniors are required by the National Curriculum to play accompaniments. *Music from 5 to 16* (DES, 1985a: 6) includes this objective for 11-year-olds: 'Accompany singing on tuned or untuned instruments by playing remembered rhythms, melodic phrases, drones, repeated chord sequences and added parts.'

How might we add these types of accompaniment to a song? It is unlikely that you would wish to include all these devices simultaneously in a song, as this would probably make it very cluttered. But you might wish to experiment with a few, or possibly include different combinations in different verses. You will have your own ideas, and so

Figure 6 Arrangement of *Three Blind Mice.*

will the children, but here are a few of mine. I take *Three Blind Mice* as my example simply because it is a song that all readers are likely to know. My full arrangement of the song is shown as Figure 6 (see opposite). Below, I describe the types of accompaniments I have added to the melody.

Remembered rhythms

Rhythms derived from that of the song itself help to ensure that the accompaniment sounds part of the song. Repetition of the rhythm of the words 'three blind mice' (**tbm**) on a woodblock throughout the song can sound effective and also have a stabilising effect. The same is true of 'see how they run' (**shtr**), which might be played on a drum. Consequently, I have combined these rhythms as an introduction to the song. After three 'three blind mice', 'see how they run' enters. And after two 'see how they run(s)', everyone starts singing. At the end of the song, the instruments continue for a little while. 'All ran after the farmer's wife' is a harder rhythm, which I have chosen to leave out for the present. I might add it when the children had mastered their parts as shown.

Drone[7]

Let us assume that we are starting the song on the note E. This means that we are in the key of C.[8] So the note C can be used as a drone, or the chord of C can be used as a drone chord. Drones can be played on any low instrument, such as a bass xylophone, but are particularly effective when played on an instrument that sustains well, such as a cello. C is one of the notes of the open strings on the cello, so this drone could be played by a cellist in the earliest stages of tuition.

Melodic phrases

As the children are to remember their parts, I want to keep them simple. Like rhythms, melodic phrases can often be derived from the melody. The phrase 'three blind mice' (notes E D C) can be repeated throughout the song. The same is true of 'see how they run' and 'all ran after the farmer's wife' but I have chosen to include just 'three blind mice', on a glockenspiel, in my arrangement.[9] I have introduced it before we start singing so that we will be able to take our note from it.

The arrangement given in Figure 6 is just one, simple, way of performing *Three Blind Mice*. I have resisted the temptation to include absolutely everything I could think of. The repeated chord sequence C G C to the rhythm of the words 'three blind mice' would, I thought, make the arrangement sound cluttered. Other parts, suggested by children or teachers, could be added, and some of mine left out. The song can be sung as a two-part or four-part round if subsequent parts start at the points marked X, Y and Z. And if you wish to go further still, note that *Frère Jacques*, starting on C, can be sung simultaneously with *Three Blind Mice*.[10] Songs that fit together like this are sometimes known as *partner songs*. As these two partner songs are both four-part rounds, the possibilities for variety are enormous. You could use word rhythms or melodic patterns from either song in your accompaniment, sing the two songs simultaneously as rounds, or make up added parts which draw on both songs.[11]

Structures such as we have considered for arranging songs can, of course, also be used to arrange pieces for instruments alone.

What about staff notation?

Staff notation is simply a means of recording some types of Western music. It is not a code that must be understood before any purposeful musical activity can take place. Some jazz musicians, and children learning the violin according to the Suzuki method, for instance, cannot read music. Some twentieth-century composers, including Luciano Berio, have occasionally found other forms of notation more appropriate to their purposes. And many musical traditions, such as Indian music and gamelan music, make little or no use of any written notation, let alone staff notation. Thus the study of written notation is not relevant to all forms of music making, and much worthwhile musical activity in any musical tradition can take place without recourse to it. Some music is not staff-notatable; other music is not notated.

Consequently, children need not be taught to read music until they are ready to use it. And once they have learnt it, it need not become the only way of recording or accessing music. Children who have learnt to read music in conjunction with piano lessons, for instance, still benefit from opportunities to compose by ear at the piano, and on other instruments. There is a parallel here with written and spoken language. Children do not learn to read and write until they have been speaking for some time. And once they have learnt to read and write, they do not stop talking to each other.

70

When are children ready to learn to read music? This depends on the music curriculum in their school, their musical experience outside school, and their own pattern of musical development. In *Music from 5 to 16* (DES, 1985a: 3), HMI state that 7-year-olds should have had:

> musical experiences which should enable them, with varying degrees of skill and understanding, to . . . associate sounds with symbols; to show a readiness to see the relationship between performed music and various forms of notation (pictorial, graphic and conventional).

According to this approach:

o Music reading is preceded by extensive experience of composing, performing and listening without notation.

o Children are not introduced to music reading before a musical need has arisen.

o Music activity without notation, and using notation other than staff notation, continues at all levels.

Teachers are not required by the National Curriculum to teach staff notation to primary children, but can of course teach it to children who are ready for it.

In *Music from 5 to 16*, the theme of *the sound before the symbol* is extended even to instrument tuition, an area of school music in which notation has been introduced traditionally at an early stage:

> Those who show the aptitude to learn recorders, violins and guitars may advantageously begin to play by ear and imitation; however, as and when there is a need for notation, it should be made available to them.   DES, 1985a: 5

A consensus that many children are ready for the early stages of music reading after about two years of sustained classroom music seems to be emerging. This means that some infants who have had systematic music education since their reception class may be reading music a little. But a teacher who takes over a class of Year 6 children who have not had sustained musical experience is unlikely to find them ready to read music before they move into secondary school.

Because music reading is not introduced until children are ready, any class will include children at different stages of music reading. Those who do not yet read music benefit from having written music

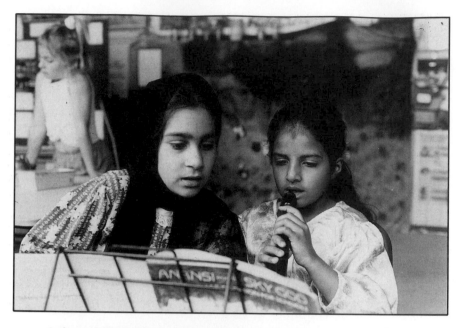

Saika and Shazia do not read music at all, but show awareness of a
potential relationship between sound and symbol by referring to staff
notation whilst they improvise on recorder and glockenspiel.

available, just as children who have not learnt to read the written word
benefit from access to written language.

Even where children have learnt to read music, music reading
forms only a small part of their classroom music. Amongst over a page
of objectives for 11-year-olds in *Music from 5 to 16*, the only references
to notation are contained within points about composing and
performing:

> . . . make a permanent record of such compositions by
> means of a tape recorder and/or the appropriate musical
> notation . . . play by ear and perform simple pieces (both
> notated and otherwise) individually and as a member of a
> group. DES, 1985a: 6

Again, the use of notation follows from music making, which continues
without it at least some of the time. Thus the sound precedes the
symbol.

Performing from staff notation is only one mode of performing;
children who perform only from it are musically deprived. Teachers
who do not read music can lead a valuable range of performing

In the school orchestra, the relationship between sound and staff notation has become explicit.

activities with children throughout the primary phase. That said, most teachers do not find music reading difficult, given sympathetic help. It can be worth getting to grips with it, if only to demystify the whole matter.

Responding to performing

In chapter 3, I wrote of three modes of responding to composing: encouraging, suggesting, and questioning. The same modes of response apply also to performing. Encouraging needs no further comment. Traditionally, much response to performing – both outside and inside schools – has been suggesting, rather than questioning. A conductor of an orchestra or choir is likely to view the interpretation of a piece of music as his or her business, rather than that of the collective membership of the ensemble. Thus the conductor will tend to issue instructions about interpretation, rather than ask individuals for their opinions.

This autocratic role of the conductor is open to question. Hans Keller (1987: 23) held the view that conductors are often dispensable.

After all, much of the music they conduct was written for conductor-less ensembles:

> The conductor's existence is, essentially, superfluous, and you have to attain a high degree of musical stupidity in order to find watching the beat, or the conductor's inane face for that matter, easier for the purpose of knowing when and how to play than simply listening to the music. But such established, collective stupidity is the conductor's very lifeblood, and it must be admitted that his attempts to maintain it at a steady level in order to justify his existence, his quick and skilful suppression of any sign of intelligence, let alone independent thought, have proved brilliantly successful . . . Under the influence of the conductor, orchestral playing has, in short, become an unmusical occupation.

Hans Keller intended to be provocative. Yet he was making a serious point. Performers who are automatons are not musicians. Thus we need to encourage children to respond to their own performance:

— This is a happy song. Did it sound happy?
— Do you think an audience will be able to hear the words?
— Did it get fast enough?
— Did any of the instruments sound too loud?

It can be difficult to answer questions about the overall sound when you have been in the midst of the performance. Listening to recordings can help. Alternatively, children can be divided into two performing groups, and invited to respond to each other's performance.

That said, there is still a need for suggesting. It is right for a teacher to share her or his greater experience with children. Rehearsals in which everyone always had their say would be interminable. And when opinions are divided, someone has to decide how to move forward. My point is simply that children can be involved in the assessment of their own performing.

One area in which teacher-suggestion becomes very important is that of deciding when an item has been rehearsed sufficiently. The adage 'practice makes perfect' is not universally valid. A teacher is usually in the best position to anticipate when the point of over-rehearsal is about to be reached. Indeed, some performances are best viewed as one-off, and not rehearsed at all.

Performing for an audience

Up to now, we have thought about performing as an informal activity taking place within the classroom. But performing, traditionally, also forms a significant part of the public presentation of the school through concerts, entertainments, carol services, and so on.

Working towards public performances can be a worthwhile musical experience for children. It can develop social skills, and enjoyment in social activity. The achievement of high standards can lead to personal satisfaction. But working towards public performances can also be boring and irrelevant. Ordinary musical activity of composing, performing and listening may be suspended whilst several weeks' work on some rather unattractive and perhaps very high songs takes place. The children may reach the best standard of which they are capable, given the material, days or weeks before the performance, and rehearsals may degenerate into a tirade about 'trying hard' and 'looking at me'. The value of children's individual contributions may be forgotten, and children with poor vocal accuracy may be asked to sing more quietly, stand behind a pillar, or play a drum instead.

The most useful public performances grow out of the music curriculum; they do not cut across it. They offer a public window into what would have been happening anyway, but provide children with an incentive to polish and focus their work. This is possible if the performance is conceived as an opportunity to show the public what children can do, rather than to use the children as a vehicle for public entertainment, and showing what teachers can do. Fortunately, child-centred performances often do entertain parents, and reflect well on teachers.

Attendance at child-centred performances can help to bring parents in touch with what their children are doing in music at school. Parents often had a rather uncreative music education themselves, and may, quite understandably, think that nothing has changed if end-of-term performances consist of performances of published pieces directed from the piano by a teacher. Inclusion of children's compositions, or items directed by children, can help parents understand the aims of the school music curriculum. Of course, some parents may experience a little initial resistance to change. The following passage is drawn from two letters which a teacher received after a secondary school concert that included children's compositions as well as works by more established composers:

A veritable mish-mash of the sublime to the rediculous [*sic*]. . .
A brief 'straw pole' [*sic*] amongst other parents following the
concert indicated a general feeling of disappointment . . . I
did appreciate the lovely plants as a backdrop but wondered
what they thought of some of the music . . . This was *not
music*, and it was a disgrace to have this offered to an
intelligent well-intentioned audience, who come to be fed
with *good* morsels . . . an excessive amount of experimental
tinkling from the classroom groups, totally inappropriate
fiddling with 'Japanese' electronic 'gadgets', and 'pop' drivel
aimed at intellectual ankle level . . . .

You can't win 'em all!

Listening

> Why is it difficult for so many people to listen? Why do they start talking when there is something to hear? Do they have their ears not on the sides of their heads but situated inside their mouths so that when they hear something their first impulse is to start talking?
>
> John Cage in *Silence* (Cage, 1968: 48)

Now we move to the final stage of the sequence

composing → performing → listening

to consider activities which commence as listening. Listening is implicit in composing and performing. But our main concern here is listening to music that is already composed, and is performed by others. But before we can embark on this, we must clear up some difficulty which has arisen in the vocabulary used by some music educators.

Listening versus hearing

There is a sense in which *listening* and *hearing* are synonyms. 'Did you hear what I said?' can mean the same as 'Did you listen to what I said?' The questioner is not just attempting to establish whether a package of sound waves has been received; she or he wants to know whether its meaning, or significance, has been registered. But there is another sense in which the meanings of *listening* and *hearing* are less similar. Hearing can be a passive act of perception, a form of reception, whereas listening always involves concentration, focus, or activity on the part of the listener: 'Did you hear the birdsong?' 'Did you listen to the birdsong?' Because birdsong is something that we can either treat as background, or engage with, *hear*, in this context, could be taken to be synonymous with *notice*, not *listen to*. The overlapping meaning of the words *listening* and *hearing* is a problem to music educators because they traditionally view the active sort of aural perception as their business, and the passive alternative as something that they wish, at least, to discourage. This verbal ambiguity has resulted in the introduction of some more obscure vocabulary to the music education literature. In *A Basis for Music Education*, Keith Swanwick (1979) writes of the musical processes of composition, performance and *audition*. In the National Curriculum, there is reference to *appraising* (DFE 1995, Welsh Office 1995). Various writers have coined the verb *to audience*. Others have referred to *active listening*. I take the view that as all listening is active, there is no need for any prefix. I use the word *listening* when I want to focus on active aural perception, and the words *passive hearing* when referring specifically to the passive sort. Use of *to hear* without qualification is in accordance with common English usage.

Music education is about active engagement with music; listening is part of music education. But what about passive hearing? It is not part of music education, but should it even be part of education? Should music be used as background in school at all? Background music is commonplace outside school. In the words of Terence Trent D'Arby: 'Music has become just another lifestyle accessory.' Roger Buckton (1988: 62) describes it as 'wallpaper[ing] our acoustic environment'. Wallpaper is something that you cease to notice after a while unless, of course, you loathe it. If we accept the validity of Buckton's metaphor, then there are two reasons why background music is inappropriate to school. First, it irritates some people. Second, its presence reinforces the habit of not noticing sound, thus making the development of listening even more difficult. Children who cannot listen, cannot engage in music, and they miss out on many other learning opportunities too.

This means that music in school has to be something special, something we notice. Whenever music is played to us, we attend to it. Music in assembly should be something we listen to, not a background for notices, or walking in and out. Music in art should be there as a stimulus, not because the sound of silence is uncomfortable. And children should learn, at least some of the time, to give music their full attention. Listening need not always be accompanied by doing something else: dancing, drawing, or writing. Music is not just a stimulus for other activity; it is an aesthetic experience in its own right.

This means that music in school will be essentially different from many children's experience of music at home. This is not necessarily a bad thing. There are many ways in which we already make conscious decisions to make a school environment different from home. We do not, for instance, often decorate classrooms by wallpapering them; we change displays frequently so as to create a visual environment that is perpetually stimulating.

A listening corner.

Listening across the curriculum

In the photograph above, Fuwad is spending his *choosing time* in the listening corner of his classroom. He has chosen a cassette of a story from a selection of recordings that includes songs and other music. As he is listening through headphones, he does not distract others, and is not disturbed himself. Provision of a second headset means that Fuwad could, if he wished, have a friend listening with him. He starts and stops the cassette, and controls the volume, himself. The weaving on display in the listening corner reflects that fact that the class are working within a topic of *Fabrics*. All around Fuwad, children are knitting, looking at fabric through a microscope, composing, writing, and doing mathematics. Some of the cassettes tie in with the topic; others do not. Later, Fuwad will make a record of his listening on the class chart.

Fuwad's class teacher believes that the ability to listen is built up in all subject areas, not just music. Listening to stories, and other children speaking, for instance, can help to build up the concentration on sound that listening to music requires. Often, the children will listen to stories and music as a class. But independent listening is important

79

too. The listening-corner environment is conducive to private, focused, listening. By checking the class chart, Fuwad's teacher learns which children are choosing to listen, and which need some special encouragement.

Listening can take place at any time; it does not require special listening material. Ask a class to sit in what they think is silence for a minute or so, and then list the sounds they notice. They are likely to include many that they would usually have ignored. Often children will notice these sounds again, even when you have not asked for silence. Listening material need not be either language or music. Try asking children to identify household or environmental sounds that you have recorded onto cassette. Invite children to bring in recordings of sounds for others to identify, suggesting, perhaps, that a sign of success will be making a recording that others *can* identify.

A vocabulary for talking about music can be developed through listening to, and talking about, individual sounds and short sequences of sounds. Often, these sounds will be produced by the children themselves, perhaps when they are experimenting with instruments (see page 32). Once concepts such as pitch (high/low), dynamics (loud/soft), duration (long/short), and tempo (fast/slow), have been learnt in an unambiguous setting, they can be applied to substantial pieces of music. But talk about music need not be limited to these rather clinical terms. There is plenty of room for personal response to music; for words chosen by teachers and children, such as 'warm', 'bright', or 'scary'.

Listening to sound and language helps with listening to music, but is no substitute for it. Neither is it something that needs to be mastered before listening to music can commence. Children can listen to music from their first day in school. Listening to sound, music and language are mutually enriching experiences.

The child as listener

What music is particularly suitable for children to listen to? When visiting primary schools, I often hear pop music or recorded extracts from popular so-called classical orchestral works: Vivaldi's *The Four Seasons*, Saint-Saëns' *The Carnival of the Animals*, Holst's *The Planets*, Tchaikovsky's *The Nutcracker Suite*, for instance. Usually, children show evidence of enjoying this music. But there is a lot more music out there waiting to be enjoyed. We could play music of any period, from any culture, written for any combination of voices and instruments.

Why is it comparatively rare for children to be played the music of a non-Western culture, or that of a living so-called serious Western composer, for instance? Teachers often choose pop music, and the music of Mozart, Tchaikovsky, and so on, because they think that children will find it particularly easy to listen to. Why? Often, teachers are generalising from their own experience. They find this music easy to listen to, and so they think that children will too. In fact, young children are more broad-minded listeners than we may imagine. Their taste for music is less predictable than we might suppose. We might think that children would prefer a movement of Mozart's *Eine Kleine Nachtmusik* to part of Stravinsky's *Rite of Spring*, or Acker Bilk's *Stranger on the Shore* to a number by the Modern Jazz Quartet, for instance. And we may be right. But we could, quite easily, be wrong.

When we say that we find some music easy to listen to, we are really saying that we know how to listen to it. We have learnt to listen to it, or music like it, over many years. We know what to expect. It is as though we have acquired spectacles through which the music we know is seen clearly. Young children have not had a chance to build up the same degree of experience yet; their response to music can surprise us. They can respond intuitively to any music.

By educating children in music, we help them to find structure and pattern in music, to hear what we hear. Provision of the closed sort of listening diet I have mentioned is well-intentioned. Teachers want children to find and pursue individual tastes. How better to start than by offering children the music that teachers like? But children who also keep alive the ability to respond intuitively to unfamiliar music remain unprejudiced listeners with greater capacity for future enjoyment of music. How can we preserve the intuitive response? Providing a wide range of listening material in school from an early age can help. Children who are aware of the diversity of music understand that the music they enjoy is just one part of a vast potential experience. They do not view the music they do not know, or do not care for, as *not-music*. They use spectacles, not blinkers.

Sam Taylor (1973) found that the music of a group of twentieth-century composers – Hindemith, Stravinsky, and Schoenberg – was more popular amongst 7-year-olds than 11-year-olds. Stravinsky's comment that his music 'is best understood by children and animals' is perhaps not as flippant as it sounds. Taylor found that adult tastes in music were well-established by the end of the junior school. So if children are to remain broad-minded listeners, action in primary school is necessary. We need to provide a varied listening diet from children's earliest days in school. All music can be appreciated intuitively on its own terms. It does not have to be approached through an understanding of the music that went before.

We are not dealing with a new problem. Adults have often had difficulty with accepting contemporary or unfamiliar music. Plato wrote, in Book 4 of *The Republic*:

> The introduction of novel fashions in music is a thing to beware of as endangering the whole fabric of society, whose most important conventions are unsettled by any revolution in that quarter.
>
> Cornford, 1969: 115

Taylor reported only children's responses to so-called classical music. But I would guess that he would have observed a similar pattern if he had played examples of the music of non-Western cultures to these predominantly white-European children. There is a case for playing music from non-Western cultures in all primary schools, not just those where there is a substantial ethnic minority population. As well as offering children wider musical opportunities, this might help to erode the widely held adult view that there is something superior about Western music, or the Western musical scale. Arguments that this scale is determined by the laws of physics are bogus. Western use of this scale is largely accidental, and Western preference for it is simply cultural.

Choosing music

There is no music which should not be played in primary school because it is too difficult. So how might we choose music for children?

Some live music is chosen simply because it is available. Live performance is more exciting than recorded performance; it is often expedient to accept almost any that is offered. Secondary-school pupils and parents are often prepared to play if invited. But teachers sometimes shy away from performing to children. This is regrettable, for children love to hear their teachers playing. Children do not compare their teachers' performance against those of renowned virtuosi: they are often impressed by the most modest performances. An

82

infant teacher learning the piano from scratch told me of the encouragement from her class as she progressed, over some weeks, from a tentative rendition of the melody of a nursery rhyme to a version using both hands.

I once attended a lesson in which a student teacher used part of a Debussy piano prelude – *La Cathédrale Engloutie* – as an illustration of loud/soft contrast. He knew the piece so well because he had learnt it as a pianist, but elected to use a recording as he was feeling a little rusty. The children listened quietly, and joined in a discussion readily. After a while, the student teacher wanted to replay a portion of the music to make a particular point. Rather than hunt round the cassette, he went to the piano and played the part he wanted. It was only about ten chords, but the children lit up, and applauded. This student now has a clearer understanding of the greater immediacy to children of live performance.

When live music is not available, how might recorded music be chosen? Sometimes, teachers wish to tie listening to some other activity. Perhaps the children are to use the music as a stimulus for dance. Or perhaps it is to be related to work within a cross-curriculum topic. Where can one look for suggestions? Your own memory is the best resource available. If you want a piece of music that will stimulate the children to dance using short darting movements, then think of a piece that would inspire you to dance with short darting movements. Choosing a piece in this way means that the piece will be relevant to you, so you will, if necessary, be able to explain to the children how you wish them to respond to it. Whatever music you choose, you may find that the children's initial response differs from your own. This is simply because composers rarely write with the explicit purpose of implying a particular type of movement.

Published listening lists are often a great disappointment. In those for topics, pieces are often classified simply by the words in the title. Under the topic *Fire*, for instance, you may find Handel's *Fireworks Music*, Stravinsky's *Firebird Suite* and the 'Ritual Fire Dance' from Falla's ballet *El Amor Brujo*. These pieces may, or may not, have anything to do with the aspect of fire that you are trying to depict. Handel's *Fireworks Music*, for instance, is ceremonial music intended to accompany a fireworks display; the depiction of fire was not Handel's main motive. Even if you happen to want some music to stimulate children to compose some ceremonial music to accompany a fireworks display, there is no guarantee that Handel's piece will do this

successfully. I doubt that Handel would have measured the lasting
success of his music by your children's ability to guess 'fireworks
display' when listening to the piece for the first time some 250 years
later.

Knowing about a composer's stimulus can, of course, inform the
way in which we listen to a piece. Penderecki's *Threnody to the Victims of
Hiroshima* takes on a whole new level of terror once one becomes aware
of the subject matter. And the fact that a piece was stimulated by the
idea of *Spring*, for instance, can be interesting and useful to children
who have just composed a piece using a related stimulus. My point is
that we should not let the supposed meaning of the music obscure the
music itself.

In *An Experiment in Education*, Sybil Marshall (1963: 189) writes
of her pupils' response to the second movement of Beethoven's *Pastoral
Symphony*:

> 'That tune's a swan', said Beverly from the floor . . . I said, 'I
> don't think Beethoven wrote a swan into it, Bev.' She looked
> up at me with eyebrows raised nearly to her hairline. 'How
> *do* you know?' she said.

Limiting our thoughts about a piece of music to some known stimulus
can limit the listening itself.

Spotting sound effects can be as distracting as searching for more
abstract images. A child attending an orchestral concert prepared
himself for Richard Strauss's *Don Quixote* by reading the programme
note. Clearly, this was going to be an action-packed performance. First
he would hear Don Quixote tilting at windmills under the impression
that they were giants, then there would be some sheep, and so on. In
the event, he missed the windmills effect, mistook the sheep effect for
creaking windmills, and then spent the rest of the performance waiting
for the sheep.

Orchestral effects such as sheep impressions are rarely effective in
any absolute sense. Their effect is relative to the sorts of sounds that
orchestras usually make. If children are not familiar with these, then
why should they recognise the sheep? And even if they do, why should
they be excited, particularly if they are in a rural school, and there are
some authentic sheep outside the window?

It is possible, and valid, to respond to music in some way that is
outside the composer's intentions. Indeed, it is possible to respond to a

84

piece without knowing what the composer's intentions are. Music chosen for use in topics need not have any explicit relationship with the topic title. Where there is some relationship, the responsibility for relevance lies with the teacher, not the composer. We cannot hold Saint-Saëns responsible if listening to 'The Elephant' from his *Carnival of the Animals* leaves children wanting to talk about pet goldfish.

As with dance, the best source of suitable music for topics is your memory. If you are working within a topic of *Growth*, for instance, think of a piece you know that grows. I might choose Pachelbel's *Canon* (see page 134). You might choose Ravel's *Bolero*, or something I have not heard of. Fine. The point is that, individually, we have taken responsibility for relevance.

What if you do not know much music? Clearly, nobody knows more than a very small proportion of all the music that could be played in a primary school. But everyone can develop a personal repertoire of listening material. You could approach this in much the same way as reading round a subject. Start from what you know and like, and work outwards, using notes with CDs, record sleeves, books, or shelves in audio shops as a guide. You may feel that there are whole fields of music about which you know nothing. Perhaps you know no pop. Perhaps you know no orchestral music, or no Indian music. Here, it is perhaps easiest to find someone who is interested in the field, and ask them to suggest three or four pieces as a starting-point. But do not feel that you need to be an expert in every field; no one can be. Children benefit from coming across teachers who have different special interests, as well as a willingness to grapple with the unknown.

An environment for listening

A recorded performance is, at best, an approximation to live music. And a classroom is not an authentic environment for listening. We cannot expect children to listen to a recorded performance in a classroom with the same enthusiasm or concentration as they would give to the same music played live at an appropriate venue. But recorded music does have one significant advantage over live music: children can listen to the same performance again and again, learning from successive listenings. And there are various steps we can take to produce a classroom environment that is conducive to listening.

1   We can choose a good-quality recording. A poor recording of a piece may help us to re-create a first-class performance we have

attended; children hearing the piece for the first time will just hear the hiss and scratches.

2   We can choose an extract of an appropriate length. It is better to leave children wanting more, than bored.

3   We can prepare the extract well. Use of a temporary cassette recording that fades in and out eliminates the disjointed listening experiences that arise when several shots at finding the right place on a record are made.

4   We can choose a suitable quiet, comfortable, environment for listening.

5   We can present music positively. Children who anticipate that they are to hear something of value are more likely to give it their full attention. If the teacher shows no respect for the music by admitting a view that it is worthless, presenting it carelessly, or talking during it, why should the children bother with it? (The prize for the most negative presentation possible must go to a teacher reputed to play organ music to his class as a punishment.)

Purposeful listening

Should children be asked to listen, or asked to listen for something in particular? There is room in the primary school for both approaches. Ultimately, we want children to learn to listen on their own, but we can guide them as they learn.

Listening can be purposeful because the music is to be used as a stimulus for another activity, or because you have asked the children to listen with some particular features in mind. You might wish to check that the children have understood some particular concept, or to find out more about their perception of the music. You might wish to know if the children can disentangle a well-known tune embedded in the music, or whether they recognise any of the instruments being played. It is difficult for us, with adult ears, to predict how difficult children may find these tasks. If we find it easy to distinguish a solo oboe sound from a solo clarinet sound, for instance, it is because we have spent a great deal of time listening to the two instruments. Children have rarely had the same opportunity. Spotting individual instruments when they are being played as part of an ensemble is even more difficult. Every instrument sound is made up of a series of harmonics at different frequencies. Just think of the complexity of the situation that you are asking the ear to unravel. There are so many ways of listening to the same piece of music. By all means encourage children to recognise the structures you perceive. But beware of assuming that a child who does not hear what you hear perceives nothing of value.

Listening throughout music

This chapter is preceded by one on composing and another on performing. As we have moved through the sequence

composing → performing → listening

the chapters have become progressively shorter. Does this mean that the sequence describes a hierarchy, with listening being the least important activity? Not at all. This chapter is concerned with only a narrow range of listening activities: those in which the listener is neither performer nor composer. Listening is a thread that runs throughout composing and performing. And because of the interdependence of composing, performing and listening, it makes little sense to talk about their *relative* importance.

But what do we mean by interdependence? Is use of the term just a pompous mode of noting the truism that composers and performers listen as they go about their business? Or is there more to it? To take the extremes of the sequence as an example, does experience in composing develop one's ability in listening to music composed and performed by others?

A few years ago (Mills, 1989b), I carried out an investigation of children's development as listeners during immersion in composing. I visited a school before and after an intensive five-week programme of composing, and, on each occasion, asked the pupils to write down what they had noticed whilst listening to a particular piece of music: 'Mars' from Holst's *The Planets*. In almost every case, the quantity and quality of the second attempts were markedly increased. In particular, many pupils had stopped writing blow-by-blow accounts, and started to note the ways in which rhythm, mood, or orchestration developed throughout the piece. As the pupils had not listened to 'Mars' in school between my visits, and were not expecting me to ask them to repeat the exercise, it seemed that the improvement was due to the experience of composing. This is some limited, but encouraging, evidence of the interdependence of composing and listening. It suggests that the listening that takes place during composing can be at least as deep as that when the focus is listening alone. In an integrated and coherent music education in which children compose, perform and listen, the boundaries between musical processes disappear. When children compose, for instance, they cannot help but learn as performers and listeners, as well as composers. That is what the interdependence is about.

PART TWO

Developing a Framework

Part One has been concerned with musical activity which is fun and for all. Where development and progression have been mentioned at all, they have been short-term concerns. How could we develop the children's response to a particular activity? Given that the children have responded in a particular way, what might we say to them, or suggest they do next?

In music, as in any other subject, short-term consideration of development and progression is a necessary condition of effective teaching. But it is not sufficient. Part Two is intended to help teachers work from first principles towards a framework for primary music that fits their particular circumstances. We start to address some issues relevant to the development of music within a primary curriculum intended to promote sustained, long-term progression and development. How do children develop in music? What might a music curriculum look like? How does the music curriculum relate to the whole primary curriculum?

In chapter 6 I approach the matter of musical development by looking at some examples of research in music education. There are, of course, no comprehensive patterns or models of musical development available. But what can the results of research – including the sort that takes place far away from classrooms – tell us about the development of primary children as musicians?

In chapter 7 I turn to the music curriculum. What are its aims? Who are we teaching? What music are we presenting, and why? I propose the idea of an entitlement curriculum intended to promote the musical development of all children without preference. How can we plan teaching without constraining children's musical development?

How can what we found out in chapter 6 inform our planning? We start with the planning of individual lessons, and then move towards more long-term projects.

As primary teachers we speak of subjects, and subject learning, less than secondary teachers. We speak rather of a primary curriculum, and often of cross-curriculum learning. How does music fit in with this? We know that there are primary schools in which music occurs only as discrete subject study. What opportunities are being missed? In chapter 8, I look at this from four oblique perspectives. First, I consider the role and organisation of music within cross-curriculum topic work. Second, I consider what there is to be gained from thinking of music as an art, not just as a discrete subject. Third, I look at some of the music that lies within a non-arts subject: science. Finally, I consider one application of music as a learning medium: the development of language.

Finally, in chapter 9, I start to look beyond the common music curriculum and beyond the classroom. In the past, school music has sometimes been a piecemeal operation centring on those children who seem particularly able as musicians. This form of organisation is incompatible with the notion of an entitlement curriculum for all children (chapter 7). I suggest ways in which school music can centre on the music education of all children whilst still offering optional opportunities for the further development of particular skills and interests.

Musical development in the primary years

How do children develop as musicians in the primary years? What can you expect of a 7-year-old composer? Is a 9-year-old ready to learn the violin? By what age should children be able to read music? Are there some musical activities that 6-year-olds do better than 11-year-olds?

Although psychological theories of learning could help us shed light on some of these questions, they would not be enough to enable us to find any answers. The questions are about musical behaviour, which is dependent on learning; none of them can be answered effectively without reference to the music curriculum that the children have been following. Just what can be expected of a 7-year-old composer depends on what opportunities for composing that child has already received, for instance. And because of the vast variation in the primary music curricula that children have followed in the past, none of these questions is currently answerable in any generalisable sense.

Other subjects may seem to have patterns of development sewn up. Looking at the Attainment Targets and Programmes of Study for mathematics in the National Curriculum (DFE, 1995), for instance, one has the impression of an agreed primary mathematics curriculum which reflects both the order in which children learn mathematics, and the ages by which children can usually learn particular pieces of mathematics. There are a number of historical reasons why there is so much more consensus about the mathematics curriculum. As many more children are examined in mathematics at the age of 16, there has been a clearer sense of purpose and direction in mathematics throughout compulsory schooling. Because of the wide use of published mathematics schemes, there has been more commonality in mathematics teaching. These are not necessarily points of which to be proud. An inappropriate model of the 16-year-old mathematician could generate an equally inappropriate top-down mathematics curriculum. Faults in a common curriculum, such as poor sequencing or low targets, would take longer to recognise because of the lack of alternative examples. Innovation requires autonomy. But primary teachers have a shared experience of mathematics teaching which they lack in music; in mathematics there is more of a basis for talking about development.

In chapter 7, we consider curriculum planning in music. Before this, we look at some research in musical development which could inform curriculum planning. This is not because ideas should always be tried and tested before they are incorporated into curriculum practice; curriculum development requires a curriculum for development. The point is that thinking about the implications of research can sometimes illuminate the process of curriculum planning, and save us going down some blind alleys.

My choice of research is highly selective, and far from comprehensive. Overviews of particular fields can be found elsewhere (e.g. Hargreaves, 1986). My purpose is to highlight a few varied studies which have produced potentially useful results, and to present each in sufficient detail for some of their implications for classroom music to become apparent. The studies chosen are drawn from publications that are widely available, and which contain other interesting and useful research. The reader whose appetite is whetted can use the references given as a basis for more extensive reading.

Research in musical development

During this century, and particularly over the last thirty or so years, psychological research into children's musical qualities has mushroomed. Early research, such as that carried out by Carl Seashore at the turn of this century, was in the tradition of psychometric testing, and took place under carefully controlled conditions. It explored research questions concerned with musical perception. What is the highest note that can be perceived? What is the smallest pitch interval that can be recognised? Do the answers to these two questions depend on age? Measurement often required the use of sophisticated apparatus, and sometimes took place in laboratories.

Research into perception continues to this day and has relevance to music education which is sometimes overlooked. But, alongside this, a tradition of exploring children's activity as musicians is developing. Here, the research questions are more directly related to composing, performing, listening and classrooms. How do children develop as composers? In what circumstances do children learn to sing in tune? And so on.

These two research traditions are not necessarily in opposition. The results of investigations in one tradition sometimes inform the questions asked in the other. Indeed, some researchers have worked in both areas at various points of their career. But because the questions asked are so different, and because the relevance of the research to music education is of a different nature, I consider the two areas separately.

Children as perceivers

Research in aural perception can be concerned with any of the parameters of sound, such as pitch, loudness or timbre. I shall focus on just one aspect of perception: pitch discrimination. This is the ability to assess that there is a difference in the pitch of two tones. Investigations of pitch discrimination often explore how close in pitch tones must be before they are judged to be the same. They may also explore whether the direction of the pitch movement can be assessed accurately. Thus an individual having his or her pitch discrimination assessed might be asked to listen to two tones and say whether the second one is the same, higher, or lower. One's ability in pitch discrimination depends on the frequency range used. Very high and very low intervals are harder to discriminate. The investigations referred to below use a frequency range in which children find discrimination particularly easy: their vocal range.

Children's pitch discrimination has been investigated by many researchers. The pattern that has emerged is as follows:

1   **Children can discriminate very small intervals**
   In 1893, J.A. Gilbert (Shuter-Dyson and Gabriel, 1981) found that children aged 7 could, on average, assess the direction of some intervals as small as two-thirds of a semitone. In the early 1960s, Arnold Bentley (1966) found they could assess one-third of a semitone. In the early 1980s, I found (Mills, 1988a) that the average 7-year-old could assess an interval as small as one-sixth of a semitone, i.e. a 1% difference in frequency. Thus several researchers have agreed that normal 7-year-olds can discriminate very small intervals. Quite how small, does not matter for the purposes of this argument. The discrepancies between the three sets of findings are probably attributable to the differing quality of the recording and replay equipment available at the time (Mills, 1984); there is no reason to suppose that the children of the 1980s necessarily have pitch discrimination any finer than those of the 1890s.

Researchers of pitch discrimination have often reported the results of work with children aged at least six years. This is usually simply because younger children might have difficulty coping with the test situation, which often requires children to write their responses. There is no evidence that younger children do not perceive fine differences in pitch. Indeed, Bridger (1961) observed that some babies aged under five days notice pitch differences of about four semitones, and they may be able to perceive much smaller intervals. It is difficult to understand how children could acquire language, and particularly accent, without some pitch discrimination.

2 **Children's discrimination improves with age**
Bentley and Gilbert both wrote of marked improvement over the junior years and into the secondary years. I found that the average 11-year-old is able to assess the direction of an interval of about a 0.85% difference in frequency. Thus the average 11-year-old ear competes with much scientific equipment for sensitivity.

3 **In any age group, there is a considerable range of ability**
This has been observed by many researchers. I found some children as young as 9 who could judge the direction of an interval as small as one-tenth of a semitone; that is, about a 0.6% difference in frequency.

What is the use of these findings? Researchers (e.g. Seashore (1938), Bentley (1966), Mills (1988a)) used the range of ability, coupled with the observation that successful performers tend to have superior discrimination, as a basis for devising musical ability tests that include tests of pitch discrimination. The generally fine discrimination of children was, if anything, a nuisance. It meant that tests had to include very small intervals if they were to differentiate between children. And very small intervals are difficult to record accurately.

But some other implications of the three points outlined above have more immediate relevance to class teachers.

1 **Teaching the concept of pitch (up/down)**
Pitch is one of the basic concepts of music. Understanding of pitch is part of the National Curriculum for infants in England (DFE, 1995) and Wales (Welsh Office, 1995). Yet many 7-year-olds do not understand it. We might suppose that a child who has yet to achieve this objective is unable to perceive the pitch differences we are presenting. Our reaction might be to present progressively

larger pitch differences to children, in the hope of finding an interval wide enough for them to notice. But as the research shows that the average 7-year-old can discriminate differences much smaller than those usually used in music, the child's problem may be labelling, not perception (see Crowther and Durkin, 1982). 'Up' and 'down' are terms associated with spatial movement. Their application to a musical context may need explanation and illustration. Teachers often approach this through the association of musical movement with spatial movement. Children may be asked to sing up a scale as they walk up some steps. They may use a hand to draw the contour of the pitch of a melody that they are listening to or singing.

Many children learn the concept of pitch easily using these sorts of techniques. Where problems persist into the junior phase, a teacher may wish to test a child's pitch discrimination using a published test (e.g. Mills, 1988a). In any case, it would be unwise to assume that a child who does not sing well in tune necessarily has any problem with discrimination (see page 65).

One question remains. If children have problems with the labelling of pitch movement, how do they manage to do pitch discrimination tests? The answer is, I think, linked with the recorded instructions that children are given as part of the test. These seem to be sufficient to enable children to apply the concept throughout the test, even if the children do not remember it, or become able to apply it on other more musical occasions. Certainly, some children who do not seem to understand the concept in a musical context display it during the test. Of course, there may be other children who would benefit from even more comprehensive instructions.

2 Coping with musically able children

The considerable variation in pitch discrimination in any age group means that some children have finer pitch discrimination than some teachers. This means that tuning tasks that are difficult for teachers are not necessarily difficult for children. A teacher is not necessarily the best arbiter of what is, or is not, in tune. This has some immediate implications. When children assert that two seemingly identical notes are different, we need to take them seriously. A child who complains that a guitar that her teacher has just tuned is out of tune may be justified. If such children are suppressed by statements such as 'it will do' or 'there's nothing the matter with it', they may not bother to listen so closely in future.

Rather, their ability can be employed to the teacher's advantage: the children can assist the teacher with tuning.

There are all sorts of musical activities in which teachers can find that some children are more able than they are. This happens to everyone, not just those who have not had much formal musical experience. The most highly qualified music graduates still find children who play some instrument or other better than they do. We have to suppress a natural reaction to be threatened by this, and instead work out how to use some children's ability to promote the development of less fortunate children, and also ourselves.

3 **Diagnosing children's musical problems**
The masking of fine pitch discrimination by difficulty with verbal labelling shows the need to think carefully about the causes of children's musical problems. Does inability to echo a clapped rhythm indicate poor rhythmic memory, or some difficulty with motor co-ordination? Does failure to walk in time with a piece of music necessarily mean that a child cannot hear its regular pulse? Musical perception takes place inside the brain; we cannot tap directly into it. If we want to know whether someone is perceiving accurately or not, we have to ask them to sing, speak, write or move, for instance, and then measure how well they do that. Any problem may result from difficulty with the singing, speaking, writing or moving itself, rather than the perception.

4 **Setting expectations for children**
The significant variation in children's discrimination is a reminder of the need to guard against setting expectations of children so low that they become unable to show us what they can do. Recognition of the dangers of underestimating children is crucial to the effectiveness of curriculum planning.

The implications I have drawn from this research are personal. I have made use of the researchers' findings according to my particular circumstances as a music teacher. Teachers in different situations may see other implications as more significant. The point is that research questions that seem not to address concerns central to music education can still yield answers that are both relevant and useful. In particular, investigation of a characteristic that is at best only a component of musical activity can have implications relevant to music education.

That said, there are many research questions that can be answered more effectively through investigation of real music making by children. We now turn to a selection of these.

Children as musicians

In this section, I focus on three studies. Each is based on children's ordinary musical activity in classrooms; in two the children are composing, and in the third they are performing. In each case, I draw out some implications of relevance to teaching and curriculum planning. The emphasis here is mine, not the researchers'. The first study, an investigation of children's sequential development as composers, culminates in the proposition of a model of composing development which may also have wider applicability. The second, an investigation of children's development as song composers, serves also as a reminder of the danger of adherence to a simple model; development is inevitably multi-faceted, and not always apparently sequential. The third, an investigation of infants' developing vocal accuracy, points to the fact that a music curriculum intended for one group of children may be inappropriate for others.

Children's sequential development as composers

How do children develop as composers? If children were all to follow the same pattern in their development as composers, then life as a music teacher would be straightforward. Given that a child had produced a composition at some particular position in this pattern, we would know where she or he was destined to move next; our job would be simply to lead the child there. As we all know, no aspect of child development – or even human development – is like that. Every model of learning is the result of some generalisation, and few individuals follow any so-called normal patterns of development literally for more than the briefest period. There are many curriculum activities in which we accept this. Although we discern general patterns of development in children's writing or painting, we learn to respond to the expressive and technical aspects of work that seems to be out of sequence. We adapt reading and mathematics schemes to suit children's individual needs by adding a book here, or missing out a section there. The idea of a sequential model of children's musical development may be attractive, but we cannot expect it to answer all our questions about response to children's music making.

In 'The sequence of musical development: a study of children's composition' (Swanwick and Tillman, 1986), Keith Swanwick and June Tillman describe a spiral model of development represented by the helix shown in Figure 7. The theoretical basis of the spiral arises from consideration of the psychological concepts of mastery, imitation,

97

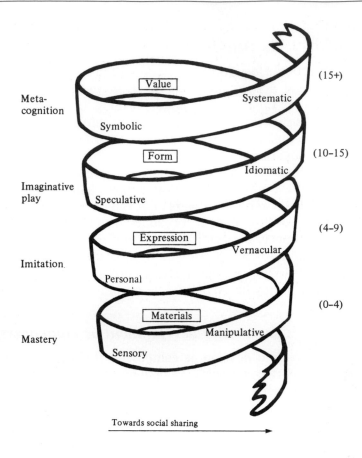

Source: K. Swanwick and J. Tillman (1986) 'The sequence of musical development: a study of children's composition', *British Journal of Music Education*, **3** (3), p. 331.

Figure 7   The Swanwick/Tillman model of musical development.

imaginative play and metacognition, and draws on the work of writers including Robert Bunting (1977), Helmut Moog (1976), Jean Piaget (1951) and Malcolm Ross (1984). The empirical evidence for the spiral arises from observation of several hundred compositions by forty-eight children taught, at various stages, by June Tillman.

The figures at the right-hand side of the helix correspond to the approximate ages at which Swanwick and Tillman believe children pass through the turns. Although only the first three turns are likely to be seen in primary school, I shall, for the sake of completeness, summarise all four. Using the explanation and examples provided by Tillman (1988: 85–86), let us follow a fictional child, Julie, as she progresses, over ten years or so, from the sensory mode, and a concern with materials, through to the systematic mode, and a concern with value.

Turn 1: Materials

SENSORY MODE As Julie explores the tone colour of instruments in a seemingly random manner, she seems to be asking the question: 'What sound does it make?'. She is fascinated by the rattle of a tambourine, and the rasping sound of the scraper.

MANIPULATIVE MODE Now, Julie seems to want to organise the sound she makes. Sometimes she beats out a steady pulse. Some of the patterns that she chooses – such as a glide up and down a xylophone – seem influenced by instrument shape.

Turn 2: Expression

Julie's concern with materials continues. But two new modes develop:

PERSONAL MODE Julie starts to show expressive character in her songs, and later in her instrumental compositions. The character is most clearly seen through changes in dynamics and speed. A song about the sun shining gets louder and faster until Julie 'almost shines herself'.

VERNACULAR MODE As Julie starts to use repeated melodies and rhythmic patterns, her compositions become shorter and less apparently exploratory. Her composition appears more derivative.

Turn 3: Form

Again, two new modes develop:

SPECULATIVE Julie starts to use contrast in her compositions. A repeated rhythm will suddenly change to give a feeling of surprise. Gradually, her use of contrast and surprise becomes more polished.

IDIOMATIC Julie works within a particular musical idiom. This may be pop or jazz, or if she has taken piano lessons she may start to compose piano pieces in a style similar to those she has been learning.

Turn 4: Value

Now two final modes are added:

SYMBOLIC Julie investigates a wider range of styles.

SYSTEMATIC Julie develops a personal and distinctive style which draws on her work in various idioms, and which she may adapt for particular pieces.

The frame of reference of the spiral is the compositions of a group of children. Yet it seems also to explain some other musical behaviour. Swanwick (1988) applies it to the account of a teenager at his first sitar recital. After some minutes of incomprehension, the teenager becomes impressed by the sounds themselves (Turn 1), then the shapes and colours they imply (Turn 2), before getting inside the structure to the extent that he becomes susceptible to surprise (Turn 3).

This is an experience that many of us have had as we start to listen to music of a type with which we are unfamiliar. To begin with, the music seems without shape, meaningless. We might wonder if the choice of notes and timing is arbitrary. Gradually, we find something that we can hold onto, even if we cannot explain what that is. Finally, we feel inside the idiom. We know what is arbitrary, and what is not. We accept the idiom on its own terms. This is the process that I likened to acquiring suitable spectacles in chapter 5 (see page 81).

We have to be careful not to generalise too far from this. A model that works well in one restricted situation, and seems to make sense in another, is not necessarily true of all musical activity. We do not know if it applies to the work of other teachers of composing, or to performing, or to all forms of listening. Neither do we know the extent to which it makes sense to superimpose composing, performing, and listening spirals, for instance, and talk about a spiral of musical development.

Curriculum planning becomes less hassle-ridden when someone else has determined the aims of your curriculum. It can be tempting to cling to the spiral, to devise curricula intended solely to promote helical progression, and to assess children mainly – or possibly only – in terms of where, spirally speaking, they are. But the evidence for the validity of the spiral in all these contexts is, as yet, slender. And some potential areas of application would appear to require development as well as evidence. The use of a spiral model for assessment is fraught with difficulty. If it is musical to revisit lower turns, for instance to absorb new musical experiences, then nobody can be assessed simply in terms of how high up the spiral he or she is.

Whilst we wait for further evidence, we may wish to think of the spiral as we try to make sense of children's music making. But this should be critical thinking; we should be testing the spiral, not using it as a frame of reference. We should also be open to other ways of thinking about children's composing, performing and listening. The responsibility for curriculum planning, teaching and assessment must continue to rest with us. Being the best model around is not enough. If we don spiral-shaped blinkers, we may miss something even better.

Children's development as song composers

Coral Davies's (1986) article, 'Say it till a song comes', offers an approach to thinking about a particular field of children's composing: song. Davies reflects on a collection of more than twenty songs composed by children aged 3 to 13. She seems not to be searching for a pattern of development so much as for a way of responding to the composition itself. Thus her approach is more reminiscent of that of Loane's (1984) work with secondary children than that of Swanwick and Tillman. Most of the children concerned were not learning to compose in any sustained way. Often, they produced their songs so that they could sing them in a play. Usually, they wrote the words first, and then repeated them rhythmically until a song emerged, repeating the song until it became stable. Davies's approach is descriptive rather than experimental, and the reader is left to come to her or his own conclusions. The main points I take away from her work are as follows.

1 **The role of adaptation within composing**
   Many of Davies's composers base their songs on material they already know. This leads Davies to argue that a rich musical experience helps with composing. Some adaptation was explicit. For instance, a 3-year-old based her song on *The Big Ship Sails Through the Alley-Alley-O*. In other cases, the influence was better integrated. Adaptation seems to be taking place earlier than would be predicted from the Swanwick/Tillman spiral (Vernacular mode). It is possible that children are more likely to adapt if they are not presented with an alternative model through being taught composing.

2 **The differing needs of children as composers**
   Davies argues the impossibility of producing a single progressive music curriculum that will suit all children. Some children arrive at school already making up songs, whilst others need a rich diet of musical experience as raw material, and possibly also specific help.

101

3   **Differing ways of assessing progress in composing**

Progress may be evident in many ways, including 'greater confidence in handling musical materials; an increase in melodic range, melodies which begin to open out rather than remain closed round the same few notes; a developing sense of shape and balance of phrases, or a more sustained, longer invention. It may be apparent in a more apt setting of words, use of more varied rhythm patterns, including syncopation, and a more imaginative turn of phrase in the words themselves.' (Davies, 1986: 288)

Davies's approach complements that of Swanwick and Tillman. She stresses the need for open-mindedness, thinking about composers and compositions on their own merits, and avoidance of prescriptive teaching. She comments on what is different, on what breaks the mould, whilst they look for what is common. The two approaches were developed in isolation; neither was a response to the other. They illustrate the differing ways in which researchers choose to make sense of what they see around them.

Singing in tune

Roger Buckton's (1988) study took place in New Zealand, but has implications of relevance to contemporary education in the UK. It consists of a survey of the singing accuracy of 49 classes of children aged approximately six: 1,135 children in all. It is difficult for a researcher to assess the individual singing accuracy of children without making them self-conscious, and consequently distressed and likely to underachieve. Buckton's approach was to devise a technique for measuring the children's singing accuracy in a situation close to a usual classroom setting. Individual children were assessed whilst singing, with their class and teacher, songs that they knew well. Personal microphones were distributed to ten children at a time. As everyone sang a song together, two microphones were switched on, with the result that two of the children were recorded individually using the two channels of a stereo tape recorder. At the end of a verse, a new pair of microphones was switched on. By the end of five verses, all ten children had been recorded. Further songs were chosen until all the children in the class had been recorded.

Buckton graded the children's singing on a seven-point scale, which ran from

'7 – sung consistently with a high level of vocal accuracy', through

'5 – occasionally vocally accurate, maintaining the general contour of the song, but singing incorrect intervals within that contour',

to

'2 – spoken, or unclear as to whether the child was speaking or singing'

and

'1 – invalid – no sound, indicating that the child was not singing, or a possible defect in recording.'

Buckton, 1988: 59.

Those children who were graded 1 (46 in all) were excluded from further analysis.

Analysis of the data shows, as usual, that the boys are less able singers than the girls. But, more interestingly, Buckton also analysed the interaction between ethnic background (as stated by the teacher) and singing grade. He found that the mean grade of Polynesian children exceeded that of European children, and that the difference in the mean singing grade of boys and girls was less marked amongst Polynesians. The results of comparing the mean singing grade of classes classified according to whether they were predominantly Polynesian, predominantly European, or mixed, were dramatic. When the 49 classes were arranged in descending order according to their mean singing grade – that is, starting with the class with the highest mean singing grade – the six predominantly Polynesian classes took first, second, third, fifth, ninth and seventeenth place. Only one of the 32 predominantly European classes appeared in the top nine.

Why is this? Were the Polynesian children receiving more systematic training in singing in tune in school? Quite the contrary. The more successful European classes *did* have systematic training. For instance, teachers provided children with opportunities to sing individually and kept records of their development. They took account of the need to find children's comfortable range, and develop confidence within this before working outwards. But Polynesian classes, though they sang a lot, did not have systematic training in singing in tune. Buckton came to the conclusion that his findings were the result of an interaction between cultural and educational factors. Singing is an integral part of Polynesian culture. Children sing with their families and in church from an early age. Fathers sing as much as mothers, so singing is probably less associated with females than it is in European culture. Children of European ethnic background, on the other hand, often arrive at school with little background in singing. Consequently, the educational needs of the two groups differ. The European children often need systematic help, whereas the Polynesian children just need practice.

What are the implications of Buckton's study for music education in the UK? It provides evidence that systematic singing tuition can help children learn to sing in tune earlier. But it also suggests that the system used needs to reflect the cultural and musical background of the children concerned. There is no one way of teaching children to sing in tune, and methods imported from other situations may be of no help. We need to work out what children's problems are, and plan accordingly.

Generalising from Buckton's investigation of singing, it would seem that matching of the task to the child is as important in music as in any other subject. We need a mixed-ability approach to music teaching. It is inappropriate to take some externally devised music scheme, apply it to all children, and hope for the best.

So how might we plan in music? This is the matter to which we now turn.

Planning curriculum music

'It's relatively easy to have a party . . .' (Ken Robinson on the
need to think beyond one-off projects when talking of an arts
curriculum)
NCC/SCDC Arts in Schools Project Conference,
Warwick, 1989

Curriculum planning takes place on a range of different levels. The curriculum may be intended for a class, a school, an LEA, or even a nation. The time over which the plan is to be implemented can vary from less than five minutes to the eleven-year period of compulsory schooling.

All curriculum planning takes place within a context of curriculum policy. The context may be defined by a complex combination of influences including government educational legislation, the curriculum policies of schools and LEAs, and the educational philosophies of individual teachers. No two teachers operate in precisely the same curriculum context; individual differences in educational philosophy result in teachers within the same school implementing their shared school curriculum policy in differing ways. The freedom of teachers to interpret external policies ensures a personal investment in the effectiveness of teaching, and facilitates curriculum development. Everyone in teaching – student teachers and probationary teachers as well as the most experienced headteacher, LEA adviser, HM Inspector or Government Minister – has responsibility for some level of curriculum planning.

Part One was about the facilitation of musical activity. Chapter 6 has provided a narrow window into children's musical development. How can we use what we know about doing and development to plan teaching? First there are some questions we must address:

- To what extent should we plan music?
- What is curriculum music for?
- What music should we teach?
- Who are we teaching?

To what extent should we plan music?

Should we plan it at all? Doesn't planning take away the magic? Shouldn't every lesson be an exciting one-off experience? We need to have the 'parties' to which Ken Robinson alluded. But parties can become rather dreary after a while, particularly if you go to them three times a week, and it's always the same old crowd, and the same loud music. A music curriculum consisting of just one-off initiatives lacks, by definition, any intentional progression. Children may have fun – for a while. But if they make progress, this is through chance rather than design. Thus some planning is essential.

We must take care not to go to the other extreme. There are all sorts of ways in which planning can become counterproductive. A step-by-step curriculum in which every possible pupil response and permissible teacher action is specified would be dangerously restrictive, and would reduce the teacher to the role of a mere silicon chip. A curriculum led by a series of objectives for children to accomplish can result in underachievement if the objectives are too easily attained. What we need is a curriculum structure which gives a sense of direction to teaching, without constraining children's progress. This is difficult to organise, particularly in a subject in which there has, perhaps, been little agreed sense of direction in the past. There are many areas – composition, for instance – in which we are only just beginning to understand what children can achieve. In this situation, it is so easy to make mistakes, like those of teachers who assume (see page 94) that a child who does not label one note as higher than another cannot hear the quality of the difference between the two notes.

There are no perfect solutions. I propose to adopt a model in which the sense of direction is determined by the overall aim of *children's development as musicians (composers/performers/listeners)*. Surely this is sufficiently broad for it not to be constraining? In order to achieve this sense of direction, we need to set out what we want children to achieve in the shorter term. I shall call plans for shorter-term achievement *objectives*, though they could be called goals or expectations. But evaluation of teaching, and children's learning, will not consist simply of ticking whether or not children have achieved objectives. We will continually be on the lookout for children demonstrating achievement beyond, or outside, what we have set for them. That way, we can adjust our current objectives, and set more informed ones for the future. Along the way, we will also find out more about what children are able to do.

What is curriculum music for?

In chapter 1, I offered some guidelines for curriculum music. Music is active, for all, and fun. These provide some pointers about the shape curriculum music might take, but offer little insight into why we are teaching music in the first place. What do we believe curriculum music offers children? In answering this question, I have in mind education throughout schooling, not just the primary phase.

The role of music in the curriculum includes the development of both expression and aesthetic awareness. Through music, children learn more about their culture. Music does not hold a monopoly on any of this. Creativity, expression, aesthetic awareness, and understanding of culture, are embedded in all other subjects as well. But music, as an art, 'offer[s] unparalleled opportunities for the development of imagination, sensitivity, inventiveness and delight – essential elements in a balanced curriculum' (Paynter, 1982: xiii). This is not all there is to say about music. Music is a way of learning. Music brings you in touch with pattern and structure. It requires reflection and analysis. So, of course, does every other subject. But music does have something rather special to offer here. Whilst you reflect on, or analyse, a piece of music, you cannot hold it in your hand, or even see it, for music exists in time; it is held only in your memory. To analyse music, you have to be able to use your mind rather like a cassette recorder: to record, play, replay, fast forward, and even rewind. The same is true of language. But music differs from language in being non-verbal. Thus music requires processes of reflection and analysis which are at least a little different from those of other areas of experience. Music enriches children's repertoire of ways of making sense of their environment. It is a crucial part of the development of the brain.

Children will take different things away from our music curriculum. Because we are teaching music, I have set an overall curriculum aim of developing children as musicians. But for some children, the extra-musical benefits of music education may be just as important as the musical ones. We cannot measure the effectiveness of our music curriculum simply by counting the number of children who go to concerts, or become professional musicians. But other possible benefits of music education, such as the development of the brain, are harder to quantify.

What music should we teach?

In chapter 5, I said that no music is out of bounds to the primary curriculum. In the past, the music heard in British schools was, almost exclusively, of a restricted – though none the less important – kind, which I shall call 'European high art'. I use this term to refer, subjectively, to the music of composers including Bach, Beethoven, Mozart and Tchaikovsky, whose many shared characteristics include the following two. First, they composed individually for an audience consisting mainly of those of high socio-economic status. Second, they transmitted their musical ideas through the use of manuscript paper.

Once upon a time, the dominance of high art in British schools might have been appropriate, or at least justifiable. If music education is about bringing children into contact with the great music of their own culture, then perhaps it makes sense for teachers to play a lot of the music that they regard as great. Today, this is not good enough. First, in a multicultural society our culture is not just European. Second, a notion that high art is great and other forms of European music are not great is open to question. Third, the transmission of our cultural heritage, whatever we mean by this, is only one part of music education.

There are really two multicultural issues involved here. First, world music is made up of different musical cultures which can be defined, in a loose sort of way, geographically. Thus we might talk about Indian music, Chinese music, or European music. Second, any of these musical cultures encompasses a spectrum of subcultures. In the case of European music, subcultures include pop, opera, and Scottish bagpipe music. This analysis does not bear much inspection. Indian music, for instance, is taking on a life of its own outside the Indian subcontinent, and pop music is not just a subculture of European music. The point I am making is that multiculturalism in music is not just about including music that originated outside Europe, but is also about reflecting the different subcultures of European music. These two dimensions overlap in a number of ways. But, for simplicity, I shall consider them separately.

British schools, traditionally, were predominantly concerned with so-called classical music, rather than popular music. Much of the music that children listened to was written by high art composers, and most of the songs they sang were classical songs, or classical-style arrangements of former folk songs. Doubtless, there were teachers all over the country who drew on pop music, but, like the teachers who encouraged all children to compose, they were regarded as quirky eccentrics until comparatively recently. The matter of whether it was appropriate for school music to be so biased towards classical music only started to receive a substantial educational airing in the 1970s. *Pop Music in School* (Vulliamy and Lee, 1976), was one of the first publications intended to publicise and promote the popular music taking place in schools. Hence, for many children, there was a huge gulf between the music they did in school, and the music they listened to at home. In some cases, the gulf was more imagined than real; it had become part of teenage folklore.

Early in the 1980s, I was regularly greeted at the school gate by a particular secondary pupil who always asked me if we were going to listen to 'Beethoven' again today. In fact, as she well knew, we had not listened to anything composed by Beethoven all year. 'Beethoven' had become, for her, a generic term encompassing all so-called classical music. Actually, we did not listen to much of that either. But, despite my attempts to use pop music intelligently in the classroom, this pupil still saw a yawning chasm between 'Beethoven', which she identified with school and me, and the New Wave which she enjoyed outside school. This pupil was not typical of her age-group; her views on many aspects of school life were extreme. And I still had much to learn about the use of pop music in school. Other teachers have been much more successful in reducing the home/school divide in music. But, to dream for a moment, would it not be preferable for there to be no divide in the first place? It cannot be eradicated overnight. But an approach to primary music in which all forms of music and music making are valued would be a step in the right direction.

There are social reasons for including non-European music in primary school; in multicultural Britain, how could a music curriculum consisting only of European music be justified? There are also musical reasons; there is much that all musicians can learn from participating in music from a range of cultures. Paynter (1982: xiii) writes: 'In education our task is to reveal the breadth of music's expressive possibilities, not to restrict them.' Swanwick (1988: 113) writes of 'inter-cultural music education', in which a range of musical styles are introduced 'not as "examples" of other cultures, with all the stereotyping and labelling that goes with such an approach, but as objects and events carrying expressive meaning within a cohesive form.'

Whenever we participate in the music of a culture to which we do not belong, we must consider the issue of authenticity. It would be wrong to pretend that we can make authentic Javanese gamelan music, for instance, on xylophones, metallophones and glockenspiels. There are many steps we can take to make our participation more authentic. These range from engaging practising musicians, through acquiring better resources, to just finding out more about the music. But inability to generate authentic participation in a particular music does not mean that we should steer clear of it. Classrooms are not authentic places for any form of musical activity. Listening to the music of Mozart takes place authentically at a concert, or at home in comfort, in response to the wish of the listener to listen. Real pop musicians do not work in classrooms, constrained by the school timetable. Yet it is still appropriate to listen to *Eine Kleine Nachtmusik* and compose pop songs in school. What is important, I think, is that we are honest with ourselves, and with children, about when we are trying to make music authentically, and when we are not. And if we are trying to make the music of a culture to which some of our children belong, we can draw them into the authenticity debate, and learn from them.

Music exists outside its culture. Swanwick (1988: 112) argues that 'It is discriminatory nonsense to say that we cannot understand something of, say, *oriental* music without understanding oriental culture, the oriental *mind.*' If we do not need, always, to be making or appraising the music authentically, what should we be doing with it? We should be listening to it, performing it, and perhaps using some of the ideas we learn from it in our composing. As part of this, we will also be talking about it. Inevitably, what we hear and what we like will be conditioned by what we already know. This is right; if every listening experience was a one-off, how could we talk about development in listening? But if we are to learn anything from music of an unfamiliar idiom, we have to make an effort to listen to it on its own terms, not just through the spectacles that we use for the music we know and love. There is no point in measuring a piece of Japanese classical music against the yardstick we usually use for brass band music. It is sometimes difficult to avoid doing this. We have, perhaps, to wait whilst we progress through the spiral experience reported by the teenager at his first Indian music concert (see page 100). This may mean waiting for a long time before we speak at all. And it may also mean letting children listen on several occasions before we expect them to say anything.

Who are we teaching?

Music is for all. We need a music curriculum which is intended for all children, whatever their musical background, race, gender, or educational ability. This is really a matter of developing a mixed-ability approach within which children are viewed as individuals, not stereotypical representatives of some particular group.

There are huge variations in the extent and range of children's musical background. It is well known that children from musically supportive backgrounds are more likely to become accomplished musicians. This will always be the case; these children have had more musical experience than anyone else. But it is nonsense to pretend that everyone else is doomed to failure, whatever that means. Buckton's research (see page 102) offers an instance of planning that was effective because it reflected children's background. We need a mixed-ability approach which enables children with little musical background to develop a firm foundation from which they may grow. Simultaneously, it must broaden and deepen the musical experience of children with more extensive background. This is a challenging notion, particularly when we reflect on the range of initial musical experience which children in our multicultural society may have. But it is one which we have to keep in mind if our claims to a mixed-ability approach are to be more than just rhetoric.

The curriculum needs to be suited to children of any cultural or racial background. This needs three forms of action. First, it requires a welcoming response to children who have not been brought up within the musical culture of the majority in their class and who, consequently, are not familiar with the material used. Second, it needs acceptance of the musical culture of all class members within the model of world music that is being adopted. Third, it requires avoidance of racial stereotyping. There is no evidence of differences in the innate musical abilities, or predisposition towards music of racial groups. Research in this area has always been inconclusive. Where differences in musical behaviour have been observed it has always been possible to attribute these to factors of social background.[1] Thus individuals living in the UK deserve to be treated as members of a culturally and racially diverse society.

The music curriculum needs to be fair to both boys and girls. In the primary school, we often find more girls than boys participating in voluntary music activities, particularly choirs. We have already seen, in chapter 4, that the lower number of boys who are able to sing in tune cannot be accounted for solely in terms of their slower physical development. In chapter 6, we saw that one explanation for boys' poorer singing might be parental role-models: fewer European men sing. If boys are to have a fair chance in music, we need to try to

111

compensate for this in school. Because of the disproportionately high number of women teachers in primary schools, there is no way that we can deluge boys with models of men singing. But we can take other steps. The first is to encourage male members of staff to sing whenever possible. The second is to avoid presenting an excessively feminine model of singing. This means avoiding songs with soppy words, and making sure that boys get just as much encouragement with their singing. Lastly, we may also be able to tackle this issue sideways. In schools where music is taught mainly by women and yet there are plenty of boys in the choir, singing is often not the only focus of the music curriculum. Sometimes there is a great deal of composing. Alternatively, there may be emphasis on instrumental performance. Boys participate in composing, and much instrumental performance, on equal terms with girls – without the handicap of negative parental role-models or developmental lag. It seems as though the musical self-esteem that develops here transfers into singing. Thus we need a balanced music curriculum.

Our mixed-ability approach to music needs to encompass children with special educational needs (SEN). All children have the right to an appropriate music education. And music can assist with the language development of children with learning difficulties. This has led to the development of teaching programmes (for example, Bulman, 1987) based on the parallel development of SEN children's cognitive, language, and music skills.

Why should music help with the development of language? Motivation may be a factor. But so might cerebral organisation. Studies of the brain have suggested that activity concerned with language takes place in the left hemisphere, and that music activity takes place predominantly in the right hemisphere.[2] There is, however, evidence that the activities of the two hemispheres can reinforce each other. Left-hemisphere stroke victims can sometimes be taught to re-develop the language centre of their brain through right-hemisphere activity such as the presentation of sung language. If a child's language centre is underdeveloped, this may be stimulated through the presentation of sung language. Naturally, this effect is not confined to SEN children. There are situations in which many individuals find it easier to recall language when it is embedded in songs.

There are two groups of children who may have some practical difficulties with music making: those with physical disabilities, or with hearing impairment. Here, I refer very briefly to some of the impli-

112

cations of their involvement in mainstream music. Teachers who have physically disabled or hearing-impaired children in their classrooms will also want to take more specialist advice.

Children with physical disabilities may still be able to play some instruments; others may require adaptation. One-handed recorders have been developed, and electronic instruments offer the possibility of an exciting range of sound played in a variety of ways. Just occasionally, one can see practice which, though well-intentioned, is not offering a disabled child the best opportunity to become a musician. I recall observing a boy in a mainstream class who had the use of only his left hand, and no prospect of gaining use of his right hand, being taught to play the recorder with a support teacher supplying his own right hand as necessary. The intention was for the boy to participate in music alongside his peers. This he did. I observed him – or rather both of them – playing *London's Burning* with the rest of the class. The problem was that the boy was never going to be able to play *London's Burning*, or much else for that matter, without the support teacher. This school had a policy that all children played the recorder. Perhaps this was why they seemed to take a sledgehammer to crack a nut. Surely, an electronic keyboard would have provided a more effective, and cheaper, solution to this boy's practical problem with performing.

In the past, hearing-impaired people have sometimes been written off as musicians. The reasons for this have often been simplistic: music is sound, and the sound reception of deaf people is limited, if not non-existent. In fact, there are many examples of successful musicians with hearing problems. Schumann suffered from tinnitus. Beethoven wrote some of his greatest works when totally deaf. Recently, deaf musicians, including some who have been deaf since birth, have been awarded music degrees, and become professional musicians.

This is not as illogical as it might at first seem, for two reasons. First, the majority of so-called deaf people have some residual hearing; technical aids can help them to make the most of this. Second, perception of music is not a simple matter of the transmission of music from an instrument through the air and our ears to our brain. The sensation we call music does not exist without the brain; it results from the conversion of sound waves to electrical impulses which the brain processes. Thus, even those with no hearing – probably less than 10% of the so-called deaf population – may be able to perceive a vibration-induced sensation which is as real as music.

Hearing-impaired people typically do not have hearing loss that is uniform throughout the frequency range. Thus some parts of the frequency range may be heard perfectly, with others being imperceptible. This can produce an effect rather like listening through a hopelessly adjusted graphic equaliser. Sounds that hearing people regard as extraneous, such as the clatter of a harpsichord keyboard, can dominate the music. Devices similar to graphic equalisers can be used to correct this problem, at least partially. Natural amplification can also be helpful: for instance, a hearing-impaired person who lies on a sprung wooden floor and listens can report a more substantial sensation.

We have been considering music in the education of children with special educational needs. Apart from the reference to language development, we have focused on music for music's sake. This contrasts with music therapy, in which the aim is therapy, and the music is present simply as a means of communication between the therapist and client. In *Music Therapy in the Education Service* (APMT, 1988: 5), music therapy is explained as follows:

> The ability to appreciate and respond to music is an inborn quality in human beings. It is well known that this ability frequently remains unimpaired by handicap, injury or illness. People who have difficulty in understanding their environment, or whose verbal communication is an inadequate form of self-expression, may nevertheless be stimulated by music and respond to it. Music therapists seek through music to arouse and engage clients, and to help them towards realising their potential.

Despite the differing purposes of music therapy and music education, the activities which take place in the two fields have some similarities. At present, qualification as a music therapist in the UK is open only to music graduates. However, recent initiatives in in-service training in some LEAs have enabled other teachers to gain further understanding of the therapeutic use of music, and to learn some therapeutic techniques.

Summary

When planning curriculum music, there are several questions which can be kept in mind:

o   What am I hoping children will achieve from my teaching?
o   Why do I want them to achieve this?

o   Will children be able to show me that they can achieve more than
     I expect?
o   Am I presenting a programme that offers breadth as well as depth?
o   Is my planning suitable for everyone present?

These questions – and their answers – provide the context for
planning. We now turn to the planning itself.

Planning a lesson

There are two main ways of planning music lessons, or indeed any
lessons. You can ask 'What do I want the children to *do* today?' or
'What do I want the children to *achieve* today?' The first, activity-based,
way of planning usually requires less thought. The teacher just reviews
the available resources – songbooks and so on – and decides what to do,
with due consideration to what the children have done before. The
second, objectives-based, way of planning usually requires more
cognitive effort. One has to think about purpose as well as activity. The
benefits of this method include the potential for a lesson that
contributes to the musical development of the children in some
intentional way. There may be some situations in which the first sort of
planning is adequate. Certainly, most of us have been driven to it
occasionally through exhaustion or lack of time. But activity-based
planning runs the risk of leading to entertainment, or perhaps
occupation, rather than teaching; it is not our concern here.

So lesson planning consists of finding answers to five questions:

1   What have the children achieved already?
2   What do I want them to achieve in this lesson?
3   How will I go about enabling them to achieve this?
4   How shall I assess whether they have achieved this?
5   How shall I avoid limiting children's achievement to what I have
     set for them?

Curriculum planning in all subjects consists of the continual
revisiting of these questions. A teacher uses them to set up a curriculum
plan for an entire academic year, but returns to them at many points
during this period, including every occasion on which she plans a
lesson. This may lead to adjustment of the original plan. But here the
focus is narrow: a single music lesson.

115

Question 1: What have the children achieved already?

If you do not know what skills, concepts and knowledge children have already learnt, what guarantee have you that your teaching will help them to develop as listeners, performers or composers? And if you do not know where the children started from, how can you evaluate their learning?

How can we establish where children are as listeners, composers and performers? We can do the following:

Consult records of their previous work
○   What was the content of their previous experience?
○   What was their response to this content?
○   What concepts and skills have they been taught?
○   What concepts and skills have they learnt?

And so on.

Question them
○   Do they understand the concepts they were taught?
○   What do they remember of their work?
○   What do they think they learnt from it?
○   What do they think they have not yet learnt?

And so on.

Observe them during musical and other activity
○   What musical skills do they display?
○   What musical skills do they fail to display?
○   What related social skills do they display?
○   What attitudes do they display?
○   What concepts are they applying?

And so on.

Exactly how you frame your questions will be influenced by the phraseology of the curriculum document within which you are working. An infant teacher who is wondering where his new class of 6-year-olds are in relation to the progression implied by his LEA curriculum document might ask, 'Can they use the words *loud* and *quiet* appropriately when describing and selecting individual sounds?' An infant teacher in another LEA implementing a school curriculum document might ask. 'Can they use a variety of beaters to make *loud* and *soft* sounds on a range of instruments?' Both of these curriculum

116

documents were devised within the context of *Music from 5 to 16* (DES, 1985a). Both teachers are investigating aspects of one of the objectives for 7-year-olds: 'to . . . be able to recognise some of the main characteristics of music – such as . . . dynamics (loud/soft).' (DES, 1985a: 3). Understanding of dynamics is also part of the National Curriculum for infants in England (DFE, 1995) and Wales (Welsh Office, 1995).

Question 2: What do I want the children to achieve?

When starting a new project, or working with a new class, your initial assessment will be wide. You will want to find out as much about the children as possible. When you come to form objectives for your teaching, you may need to cut down your field of activity considerably. It is just not possible to tackle all areas of composing, performing and listening simultaneously. How you do the cutting down could be based on several considerations, for example:

○ Long-term balance between listening, composing and performing.
○ The children's preferences.
○ The need to respond to individual differences.
○ The priorities expressed in your curriculum document.

Objectives state the purpose of teaching. Musical objectives are concerned with children's development as listeners, performers or composers. An infant teacher might set the following objective for a series of singing lessons: 'The children will be able to sing several songs roughly in tune with me.' When setting this objective, she need not specify the songs that the children will attempt to sing. The mastery of material, in this case a series of songs, simply provides the means of accomplishing her objective. Materials are chosen in response to question 3.

Question 3: How can I enable the children to achieve the objectives?

Once we know where children are, and have decided where we wish to take them next, we are free to determine the process and content that we will use to do this. In other words, we are ready to plan the lesson itself. Usually, we will wish to set the activities intended to achieve our objectives in the context of a lesson which gives children an opportunity to warm up, allows for development and consolidation of learning, maintains children's interest, and so on. This aspect of planning is not subject specific; we focus on the music activity itself.

117

There are always several ways in which a musical objective may be accomplished. Our choice of approach depends on many factors, not least the extent of our own musical expertise. Teachers with extensive formal music skills usually have more choice of approach, but rarely a greater chance of success. As examples of this point, I have chosen two of the objectives for 11-year-olds stated in *Music from 5 to 16* (DES, 1985a: 6). Both of these examples are relevant also to the National Curriculum in England (DFE, 1995) and Wales (Welsh Office, 1995). In both cases, I suggest a range of approaches intended to move children towards accomplishing the objective.

Example 1

'To know from memory and be able to join in with songs for assembly'

APPROACH 1 Teach Parry's *Jerusalem*, accompanying the children by playing Parry's very difficult piano part.
APPROACH 2 Teach Parry's *Jerusalem*, with the additional support of a visiting pianist.
APPROACH 3 Teach the children a song that you can accompany on the guitar.
APPROACH 4 Teach the children a song that needs no accompaniment.

Note *Music from 5 to 16* does not specify that children need to learn *Jerusalem*, or indeed any other named song. Children who have not learnt *Jerusalem* by the time they enter secondary school can hardly be said to be culturally deprived. If you think that *Jerusalem* is an appropriate song, and are able to play the piano part, or have a colleague able to help you out, then go ahead. Otherwise, choose a song that is within your capabilities as an accompanist, or which sounds better without an accompaniment. You will still be working towards the same objective; the children will not lose out.

Example 2

'Be able to recognise the various elements of music such as . . . chord . . .'

ALL APPROACHES Start work on this objective by drawing children's attention to the differences between chords and notes played in isolation. First explain that a chord consists of two or more notes played simultaneously. Continue with one of the following approaches.

118

APPROACH 1 Play some random chords on the piano. It does not matter how strange they sound. Occasionally play single notes. Check that the children can hear when you are playing a single note, and when you are playing a chord.

o Give them some difficult examples, for example a chord consisting of two notes an octave apart.[3] Play some chords of two, three or four notes, and ask the children how many notes they can hear. Demonstrate the correct answer by building up the chord note by note.

APPROACH 2 If you play folk guitar at all, use your guitar. Play the children some chords you know – perhaps D major[4] and E minor – and check that the children can distinguish these from single notes.

o If you are able to, play some octave chords as suggested above for the piano. Play some invented chords; again, it does not matter how strange they sound. If you are able to, demonstrate several major chords. Ask the children to distinguish between major and invented chords. Repeat for minor and invented chords. Finally, try major and minor chords.

APPROACH 3 Use an electronic keyboard, or synthesiser, that has chord buttons. Repeat Approach 2 using the chord facility to provide automatic chords. Play single notes.

o Play invented chords yourself on the keyboard.

Possible extension for teachers using any approach who are able to harmonise simple melodies by ear.

o Explain that the chord of C major consists of the notes C, E and G in any order, and that the chord of G major consists of the notes G, B and D in any order. Divide the children into five groups, one for each note, and organise the playing of the chords. Use the chords to accompany a simple melody, for example *Three Blind Mice.*

Note
All these approaches exceed the requirements of the Example 2 objective (from the points marked o). The objective does not, for example, specify discrimination between particular types of chords. Thus children can be offered the opportunity to work towards this objective by teachers who do not know how to work out which notes are in the chord of D major, for instance.[5] In fact, teachers who do not know the so-called rules of harmony often approach this objective more imaginatively. *Cognoscenti* can be inclined to restrict themselves to the

official chord forms that they know, for example major and minor chords. This gives children a limited, and culturally biased, idea of the range of sounds encompassed by the term 'chord'.

These are just two examples of the ways in which teachers can take into consideration their own musical expertise when deciding how to facilitate children's accomplishment of curriculum objectives. This principle can be applied to all the objectives for primary music in most of the recent curriculum documents I have seen, and also to the National Curriculum. I repeat a point that I made earlier because I think it is so important: teachers with extensive formal expertise often have more options concerning the means they can use to accomplish curriculum objectives, but they do not hold a monopoly on successful curriculum implementation.

Question 4: How shall I assess whether the children have achieved the objectives?

Often, objectives can be turned into a question form. An objective: 'The children will learn to maintain a steady beat for a short while without help' is easily turned into the question 'Can the child maintain a steady beat for a short while without help?' This is not a very precise question. How steady is *steady*? How long is *a short while*? How much help will the child get in starting the beat, and what speed will the beat be? Within the present context – the setting of objectives for an individual lesson – I do not think this matters. We are not trying to set a national standard of *steadiness*. As the teacher makes assessments of the children's achievements, he or she will develop standards to suit that teacher's purpose. The teacher might be particularly interested in what *all* the children are able to do, and what, perhaps, only ten children can do. One teacher's standards may not be exactly the same as the teacher's in the next room, but then the assessment is not being made with the purpose of comparison between the two classes.

The need to use seemingly woolly questions for assessment is even more apparent when the children have been involved in a more complex activity, perhaps composing. An objective for the children, 'To learn to use contrast within their compositions', for instance, may result in a question such as 'Can the children use contrast in their compositions?' How much contrast? What sort of contrast? Is the use of contrast to be well integrated, or is it all right for it to stick out like a sore thumb? Again, the teacher is not asking this question as part of a national survey of contrast within composition. The personal validity with which she or he applies the question is sufficient. And the teacher does not need to answer the question with a simple 'yes' or 'no'. Responses may include 'Yes, but the group's compositions have now become very disjointed' or 'I do not know. His piece started slow and ended fast, but I am not sure whether this was intentional or not. I think he says it was intentional just to please me.' In both these cases, the teacher's responses will help him or her to set future objectives. Thus the purpose of the assessment has been fulfilled. The teacher may choose to set more refined objectives which are more amenable to assessment in the future. There is no point in setting objectives that are any less clear than necessary. But hopefully this will never end up with the tail (assessment) wagging the dog (teaching). It is far better to have some slightly inexplicit questions that make sense to the teacher and deal with music as a holistic experience, than to set only clinical objectives which could be measured by a machine and have little to do with music.

Question 5: How shall I avoid limiting children's achievement to what I have set for them?

That we structure children's experience by teaching them at all reduces the directions in which they can develop. But we believe that by teaching children we open new doors to them which they would not have opened, or even located, for themselves. Thus the business of not constraining children's achievement is, in a sense, a damage-limitation exercise. But there are several constructive steps that we can take. First, we can keep our eyes and ears open. When observing children making music we need to notice the things they do that are outside the objectives we have set. We need to see and hear the child who may or may not be achieving an objective of 'composing short melodies on a tuned instrument' but who is showing an astonishing facility in playing a xylophone. 'What else did I notice?' can become a routine part of the evaluation of children's learning. Second, we can set open-ended assessment questions which enable children to show they can do more than we think. 'Can the child maintain a steady beat for a short while without help?' might enable a child to show she can do this at a variety of speeds including some slow ones which we might have thought were too difficult. Third, we can vary our styles and modes of teaching from time to time so that children have a variety of opportunities to show us what they can do that we have not asked for.

Planning for the National Curriculum in music

The previous section refers to short-term planning: just one lesson. It concerned a teacher planning for his or her own class, and working within the context of a curriculum scheme that is already defined. Now we move to consider planning on a larger scale: the production of a school music curriculum scheme which meets the requirements of the National Curriculum (NC) in England or Wales.

All maintained primary schools in England and Wales will teach an NC in music (DFE 1995, Welsh Office 1995). The first version of the NC was introduced to pupils in Year 1 and Year 3 in September 1992, and the new 1995 curriculum will be in place throughout the primary age range by the summer of 1996.

The form of the NC in music (and also art and PE) differs from that of other foundation subjects. In other subjects – English, mathematics, science, technology, history and geography (and, in Wales, Welsh) – primary teachers are required to teach Programmes of Study (PoS), and assess the achievement of pupils against nine-level descriptions for each attainment target (AT). In music, the level descriptions are replaced by End of Key Stage Descriptions (EKSDs) against which pupils must be assessed at the end of Year 2 and Year 6. Moreover, the music PoS leave teachers considerable freedom concerning the content of their curriculum. For instance:

o   Children are not required to perform, or listen to, the music of any named composer.
o   Although it is expected that children will learn to play a range of instruments, the only named instrument they must all use is their singing voice.
o   Primary children are not required to learn to read music from staff notation.

Thus teachers can develop a music curriculum that meets the musical needs of children, and exploits the differing musical strengths and interests of teachers within their school.

In England, there are two ATs: performing and composing (AT1) and listening and appraising (AT2). For assessment purposes, AT1 carries twice the weight of AT2. In Wales there are three ATs: performing (AT1), composing (AT2) and appraising (AT3). Thus the basic balance of the music NC is the same in England and Wales,

122

though there are some significant differences in the PoS and the EKSDs. In both countries, the PoS and EKSDs for each AT are stated separately, but teachers are, of course, free to teach across ATs.

As well as the statutory PoS and EKSDs, the NC includes examples of music activities which illustrate the PoS. For instance, parts of the PoS (for England) are illustrated with the examples 'add a percussion part to a song' and '[use] names for pitch such as C, G, doh, soh'. These examples are all non-statutory; teachers may adopt them, or not, as they think appropriate. The first example describes an activity that many teachers have found worthwhile over the years; it is likely to be adopted widely. However, teachers who do not wish to introduce pitch names including C, G, doh and soh, either because they do not judge it appropriate, or have not learnt to use these names fluently themselves, can ignore the second example without jeopardising their coverage of the PoS.

The same principle of discretion applies also to the non-statutory guidance (NSG) issued by the National Curriculum Council (NCC, 1992) for teachers in England, and by the Curriculum Council for Wales (CCW, 1992) for teachers in Wales. Teachers may find aspects of their NSG, or that relating to the other side of Offa's Dyke, helpful. But they cannot be held to task for deciding not to implement it provided, of course, that they are meeting effectively their statutory requirements.

Devising a school curriculum document is rarely a matter of starting with a blank sheet. Usually, the school already has a music curriculum which will be developed. How might one go about this? Reflection on the current curriculum, its aims, its strengths and weaknesses, its coherence, what is missing, what is there that cannot be justified, and so on, can be a useful first stage which draws in everyone involved. This may result in agreement that the current curriculum plan needs little revision. Perhaps just a little fine tuning is needed to update the use being made of information technology or to strengthen progression within composing. Suppose, however, that it is agreed that a complete rethink is needed. What issues should be addressed? Many of the points considered in the section on lesson planning apply here but on a larger scale. In addition, the ways in which the curriculum will be adapted by teachers of differing musical experience may need to be spelt out. The PoS must be covered, and children must be given opportunities to demonstrate their achievement against the EKSDs. Below are some further matters for consideration.

123

Finding a feasible approach to curriculum planning

There is no one ideal way of writing the curriculum for your school: there are millions of feasible ways, and you just have to find one of them. An approach different to yours may be better, or may just be different. A decision that you might need to make early in your planning is whether to try to build your curriculum 'top-down' from music activities which you know from past experience are coherent, progressive and exciting, checking your coverage of the PoS and focus on the EKSDs, or 'bottom-up', by starting from the sections of the PoS, sometimes known as strands. My view is that the top-down model is likely to be more successful for two main reasons. First, it enables you to capitalise on activities and approaches that have worked well in the past. The NC is intended to describe existing good practice, not a completely new sort of practice, so you should not need to throw out all of your previous work! Second, the top-down model is more suited to the nature of music, and the structure of the music NC. In contrast to some other foundation subjects, notably mathematics and science, the music ATs and PoS sections divide up the subject primarily according to process, not content. The bottom-up approach can lead in music to a fragmentary curriculum which fails to exploit the close relationships between the processes described in different PoS sections. Whilst it makes sense to teach scientific content about electricity and sound (science AT4), for instance, on separate occasions, it makes less sense to set up music activities which, for instance, teach children to 'sing songs from memory, developing control of breathing, dynamics, rhythm and pitch', without also taking the opportunity to help them learn to sing unison songs . . . developing awareness of other performers, another section of the PoS for AT1 in England. Indeed, it makes a great deal of sense to aim to work across much of the range of the NC for most of the time.

Balancing the curriculum

Performing, composing and listening/appraising all need high profiles in the music curriculum because they are the three fundamental activities of musicians. Moreover, teachers are required to assess children's achievement in each of these activities towards the end of each Key Stage. Hence we talk about balancing the curriculum. But this does not mean that equal time allocations need necessarily be given to composing, performing and listening. This may be an effective way of organising balance. Equally, it may not. What is needed is an adequate amount of time to listen, compose and perform properly. The planning team will need to make their own decision about what this means. To give an example from elsewhere in the curriculum, is it more important that a child should be able to cross a road safely, or that she should be able to catch a ball? Most people would agree that being able to cross a road safely is at least as important as being able to catch a ball. So why do children spend more of their time in school catching balls, rather than practising road safety? Mainly because it is generally agreed that children can be taught road safety in less time.

The same point applies to the time allocated to sections of PoS. Even if teachers were required to weight evenly children's achievement in each section, it would not follow that equal amounts of time should be devoted to them.

Teachers who recall the heavy media attention given to the place of history and appreciation of so-called classical music in the NC for England may be surprised to see how few references there are to this matter in the PoS and the EKSDs. Clearly, the NC is essentially practical. In Wales, the emphasis on practical music-making is even more pronounced.

In England, there is a requirement that children listen to the music of some 'well-known' composers and performers. There are no set works and no set composers. When planning this part of their curriculum, teachers may wish to include amongst their composers some who have influenced the development of music making, or who are well known, in the community in which they work. All children in England and Wales will need to listen to a broad range of music written in different times and places, and for different purposes, including some so-called classical music, but the balance between Presley, Puccini and Polish folk song, for instance, will vary from school to school.

125

Meaningful progression

As well as their freedom over content, teachers have more freedom concerning progression than in some other foundation subjects. Teachers have the task of deciding how to move infants, over a period of two years or so, towards the first EKSD, and how to move juniors, over four years, towards the second one. There are many ways in which children could be encouraged to progress as musicians; it is likely that different schools will reach differing conclusions. However, the progression that teachers need to build into their teaching, and into children's response, must be musical progression. Children must become progressively better composers, performers and listeners. Progression in composing, for instance, is achieved through making greater demands of children as composers – by helping them to become better at organising sounds, and patterns of sound, to produce compositions. Children who have composed in response to a wide range of stimuli from their earliest days in school often make substantial progress as composers of their own accord. The matter of deciding how to move them still further forward often becomes much clearer when they are present, and composing (see page 47).

When planning for progression, we often structure learning so that it moves from the simple to the complex. We teach children to count before they add. We teach them to add before they multiply. We teach recorder players to play at least one or two isolated notes before we move on to melodies.

Progression from simple to complex often makes a lot of sense. But not all learning is amenable to this sort of organisation. Some learning takes place holistically. A word may be read at sight, rather than as a combination of letters. A painting may be appreciated, at least initially, as a whole, not as a combination of brush strokes. A piece of music may be responded to intuitively. We would not think of expecting children to understand all the components of a piece – the structures, techniques and concepts it embodies – before we played them the piece itself.

Simple to complex progression is effective only when the constituent steps are meaningful. In music, this means that each step must be musical. Otherwise, breaking learning down into supposed simple units can result in children being asked to develop skills that are unmusical, and which may actually have to be unlearnt before the child can progress. Percy Scholes (Arnold, 1983: 432) summed up this problem in a comment on the use of associations between individual notes and colours to promote music reading:

> . . . there seems to be little to be said for the practice, which, apparently, is merely an illustration of the way in which ingenious and kindly teachers often complicate comparatively simple subjects by inserting unnecessary steps.

Allowing young composers to use only the usual pentatonic scale (see page 46) is another example of well-intentioned, but inappropriate, structuring of learning. Once children find that they do not have enough notes to play the melodies they know from the world outside, they may stop playing by ear. Having found that nothing sounds dreadful in this pentatonic scale, they may stop listening to what they compose. Consequently, when children are finally allowed to use any notes, they have to relearn listening and playing by ear. In other words, initial pentatonic composing does not simplify composing in any musical manner. In the longer term, it makes composing more complicated than necessary.

Of course composing is learnt progressively, and the teacher can provide structure, in a musical sort of way, to promote progression. But this can start from some observation of where the children are as composers, followed by thought about how they might move forward. If the children seem to be confused by having too many notes, then try cutting them down occasionally – but not necessarily to a pentatonic scale. Would we try to develop children's writing by restricting the letters or words they had available for months on end? Imagine a school where the infants use only blue paint, with red being introduced at the age of 8, yellow a year later, and mixing at the age of 10!

A related problem arises when young children are given only a narrow range of instruments on which to compose and perform, and then introduced over several years to instruments which they could well have been playing since they were toddlers. In particular, young children are occasionally denied access to instruments that can produce loud, as well as soft, sounds (e.g. cymbals), instruments that produce low sounds (e.g. bass metallophones), or chromatic instruments – that is, instruments which include the piano black as well as white notes. I have never heard a convincing musical argument for this practice. Young children have no difficulty working with a wide range of dynamics, pitch and notes. Five-year-olds are not too young to start learning to select a dynamic range appropriate to the task in hand, to practise discriminating between low notes, or to pick out or compose melodies that use black and white notes. If children are denied this experience in school, this simply increases the advantage of those who have it at home. They are less likely to become confused when the

127

chromatic xylophone first appears when they are 7, or to go berserk when they get their first chance to hit a cymbal at the age of 8, or to say that they cannot hear the difference between low metallophone notes first presented when they are 9. They do not suffer the dips in their progress which are almost inevitable for less fortunate children.

A further example of inappropriate structuring is the provision of a listening diet that excludes contemporary so-called serious music (see page 80). Here, children are deprived, on grounds of supposed simplicity, of some music which young children, as open-minded listeners, do not seem to find particularly difficult. But by the time children are introduced to contemporary music, they have developed a taste which excludes it: they have to relearn open-minded listening. Listening to some music has been made more difficult, in the interests of simplicity.

In all of these examples, an attempt at simplification causes a dip (or U-shape) in progress at some later stage. U-shaped behavioural growth has been observed in children's development in many fields. It is used to account for children's, at least temporary, loss of apparent artistic flair as they become preoccupied with representational drawing (Gardner and Winner, 1982). It may be that dips are sometimes an inevitable part of progression. Progress may sometimes have to halt whilst a child grapples with a new concept that he or she could not have accommodated earlier. But going through dips is unpleasant, time-consuming, and potentially demotivating. There is no point in instituting unnecessary dips. Sequential learning has its place in music. But sequence should be derived from some sort of natural, musical, progression. It should not involve children in learning misinformation, disinformation, or unmusical skills which have only to be unlearnt later. Nor should it constrain the musical growth of children at any stage in their school career.

Meaningful assessment

Teachers in England and Wales have received descriptions (EKSDs) intended to help them assess the achievement of children at the end of Year 2 and Year 6. Supplementary guidance on assessment and reporting may be issued. Indeed, teachers in Wales have nine-level descriptions which they may use if they wish. It would be possible in principle to use the EKSDs as a shell for reports for individual children, such as the following for a 7-year-old in England:

128

Ahmed enjoys singing with a group of friends, and knows over 30 songs from memory. He handles instruments with care, and is learning to use beaters better when playing xylophones and metallophones. He shows a good sense of pulse when accompanying the singing of his friends. He shows imagination when exploring the sounds which can be made with instruments, and chooses the instrument sounds which he will use in his compositions with care.

He listens attentively to recorded music, and is learning to talk about it using musical terminology.

However, this would clearly be very time consuming, and might not give a realistic overall picture of Ahmed's musicianship, because the EKSDs are so heavily stranded.

While teachers wait for guidance, it makes sense to find a time-effective way of recording the assessments of individual children which they make routinely during lessons, or as they reflect on lessons. In practice, a great many of these potentially valuable assessments are lost, for lack of teacher time. Recordings on cassette or video are effective ways of logging significant performances or compositions which teachers knew were about to happen. Children's and teachers' evaluations of their work can be included, if appropriate, on the recording. However, much worthwhile achievement is displayed less predictably, when the recording equipment was switched off. Consequently, a written system of logging achievement as it arises can be helpful. Systems which simply record achievement as it occurred are easier to use than complex tick lists based on NC strands, for instance, and often give a more rounded picture of children's developing musicianship. Perhaps the simplest method of recording is to make notes of achievement by individuals on removable self-adhesive labels (ie Post-its), which are later stuck onto a single sheet of paper for each child. The sheet could be initially blank, or perhaps divided into sections such as composing, playing, singing and listening/appraising. Example of records could include:

Jake 5/2/96
Sang Humpty Dumpty unaccompanied to the class. His idea. A beautiful performance.

Akram 7/12/95
Recognised Ravel's Bolero from the opening few bars. Only child in class to manage this.

Belinda 10/1/96
Joined in singing during assembly. Not seen her do this before.

Tom 13/2/96
Solo keyboard composition recorded on class cassette. Ostinato in left hand, improvised melody in right hand.

Clearly, no teacher will have time to log the achievement of all the children in a class in this detail at the end of each music lesson. But if each music lesson resulted in an average of only three Post-its, and many teachers will manage a higher average, some worthwhile records would still emerge. When deciding which children to write about, it may be helpful to focus on those demonstrating achievement that seems to be new for them. It will be possible to tell which, if any, children are seemingly invisible in music lessons by looking for empty pages among the individual records, perhaps a couple of times each term. Achievement which arises outside class lessons, for instance during lunchtime clubs or instrumental lessons by peripatetic teachers, can be logged onto children's records in the same way.

These records could serve a range of purposes. They could be passed as they are to a new teacher at the end of a year, or in photocopy to a teacher at a new school, or to parents. They are likely to provide teachers with much of the evidence that they will need when using the EKSDs.

Implementing a curriculum plan

Curriculum plans always leave room for some degree of flexible implementation. Midway through realisation of a plan, an unpredicted response from a child can lead to a change in direction of teaching. This may be a minor detour, or a complete change of route. It may lead to minute adjustment of aims, or a complete rethink of purpose. Planning, preparation, and experience, all help a teacher to capitalise on children's response in a way that is likely to be productive. But they never result in a teacher being able to determine exactly how a lesson, let alone a longer period, will run.

I tend to think of the aims of curriculum planning in music as a series of layers, rather like those of an onion. The outer layer is the most abstruse, and yet the most important. It is to do with children's overall development as musicians: as listeners, performers and composers.

130

Moving inwards, subsequent layers define musical development in terms that become progressively more immediate. A layer close to the outer layer might be to do with aims for the year. Moving further in, we have the aims for the term, and then finally those for the lesson. Each lesson is planned within the terms of all these other layers. When children's response to a lesson surprises us, we break out of the immediate layer into a higher-order one so as to maintain overall musical development. A plan for a series of compositions about the seasons may be abandoned when the first composition, *Winter*, shows an exciting use of timbre which we want to develop without the constraint of thinking about summer. A plan to work on a Hallowe'en composition over several weeks may be discarded when the stimulus fails to set the children alight, or they quickly produce a work which is complete, though perhaps not on the grand scale we had anticipated. Ultimately, what matters is children's musical development, and we can sacrifice elements of our more closely defined musical concerns in order to achieve that. John Paynter sums this up:

> I have to say, in the end, I think that all that matters in music education is that what we do is musical. I don't care what it is. I would applaud whatever was happening in a classroom provided it was actually involving children in musical experience.
>
> Salaman, 1988:31

Beyond the layer I called musical development is a still more fundamental one – perhaps the onion skin – of development in general. As primary teachers we are concerned with all aspects of children's development in school. Music is a special and crucial part of this, but still only a part. In chapter 8 we set music in the context of the primary curriculum.

Music within the curriculum

In this chapter, we set music in its wider context – the primary curriculum – and consider four of the issues this raises. First, we look at music within whole curriculum initiatives: topic work, or thematic work, as they are sometimes called. In the past, music has appeared within topics less frequently than some other subjects (NCC, 1989). I take the view that what is good for other subjects is probably good for music too, and give some examples which show the range of possible approaches to music within topic work. Second, we consider music as an element of the arts. What is there to be gained from thinking of music as an art, not just a subject in its own right?

Dividing up the curriculum into the arts, the humanities, and so on, can result in an illusion of watertight compartments. As music is an art, we might be tempted not to think about music when teaching outside the arts. In fact, there is music, or the potential for music, everywhere. In the third section, I take a particular example of this by looking at some of the music that lies within science. Finally, I touch on the use of music as a means to another end. How can music be used as a learning medium? I take a particular example: music in language development.

During this chapter, we return on several occasions to one dominant theme: the musical purpose of musical activity. However we are thinking of music at any particular time – as a subject, an art, an element of science, or a learning medium – the music can be done musically. Even at times when our first priority for a child is not musical development, but learning to read, or scientific understanding, the music can be organised so as to take children forward as musicians: as composers, performers or listeners. Cross-curriculum work is about enrichment, not compromise.

Music in topic work

Music, as we shall see, could be involved in topic work in many different ways. But, often, it is not there at all. Why is this? If we believe that cross-curriculum work is a viable approach to the primary curriculum, why should music be left out? Usually, music's exclusion from topics is just a matter of habit. Here, my intention is to show the range of possible approaches. Whether music *should* feature in any particular topic is a decision that a teacher will make after due consideration of topic coherence, and whether the children's current musical needs are best responded to within or beyond the topic. My purpose is to show that music *could* be involved in any topic. Music can be organised as flexibly as any other subject.

Schools and teachers differ in their approach to topic work. Sometimes the topic *is* the curriculum; in other cases the topic serves as a temporary focus, with some work in most subject areas taking place outside it. Whatever the approach, music can take the same role as other subject areas.

Music's role in topics can sometimes be a little tokenistic. Whereas the contribution of other subjects to the topic has been carefully thought out with a view to children's development in the subject and throughout the topic, music may consist simply of listening material or songs chosen because of some relationship between the title and the topic. Songs and listening material can form part of a useful approach, but only if there is a musical reason for them being there. We need to be able to justify planned musical activity in terms of children's anticipated development as composers, performers or listeners. The musical activities available are much wider than just songs and listening material with the right title. Any activity that we might think of including in a music lesson is, in principle, open to us. What is needed is musical *and* topic-related validity.

Below, I give some examples of activities that took place as part of music's contribution to various topics. Described without the context of their topics, they may sometimes sound contrived; in practice they were not. This list is not intended to provide an agenda for music in any topic you might think of. It is only a selection of the possibilities. In any topic, some activities are more appropriate than others. The list is intended simply to act as a stimulus for your own ideas.

A game

EXAMPLE TOPIC: *Dinosaurs*

The children played a board game based on a published game, *Prehistoric Ramble.*[1] Whilst the die was thrown, the class sang a special dinosaur song. Some squares on which the counter might land have

133

instructions for a composition to describe a particular species of dinosaur. The teacher adapted the game by reducing the number of dinosaurs, rewriting some of the composing instructions to reflect the language level of her Year 3 class, and replacing the published dinosaur song with one that the class already knew.

Performing

EXAMPLE TOPIC: *Growth*

The class sang *The Runaway Seed* (see page 66), a song with words written by their teacher.

EXAMPLE TOPIC: *Time*

The class sang *Ticking Clocks*,[2] a published round which includes fast and slow ostinati.

Listening

EXAMPLE TOPIC: *The weather*

The class listened to the storm sections from each of the following pieces:
Richard Strauss: *Alpine Symphony*
Britten: *Four Sea Interludes*
Rossini: Overture to *William Tell*
Grieg: *Peer Gynt*
These extracts were chosen because the composer's stimulus lies within the topic *and* the teacher is convinced that the extracts are storm-like. Thus she presented them positively and, had the children not heard the relationship with storms, would have been able to explain why she found them convincing. She chose not to play the storm sections from Vivaldi's 'Summer' from *The Four Seasons*, or from Beethoven's *Pastoral Symphony* because she finds them less convincing as storms.

EXAMPLE TOPIC: *Growth*

The teacher played a recording of Pachelbel's *Canon*. Pachelbel is not known to have written this piece in response to a stimulus of growth. However, it audibly grows. Because the piece is a canon, it starts as a simple melodic line, with the other parts entering progressively. Thus, a multi-layered structure grows. The feeling of growth is strengthened by the tendency of later sections to include faster melodic

134

patterns. The teacher feels a particular aesthetic response to this piece. She describes this by saying that, to her, the music has become more than the sum of its parts. She uses the analogy of a growing onion: the layers developing as the onion grows correspond to the new melodic entries. But the onion is an entity, not just a series of layers.

The children became very fond of this piece too, and often asked to hear it. After they had heard it several times, the teacher talked a little about the onion analogy. Explaining this too early might have rushed the children into hearing the piece only in the way that she does.

Composing

Composing is a highly adaptable activity. Whenever it is appropriate for children to be engaged in creative writing, they probably could be composing.

EXAMPLE TOPIC: *Fire*

After sitting by a real fire on a cold, dark day, and following a discussion, the children were asked to compose a piece entitled *The Real Fire.* The groups chose to emphasise some different aspects: the flickering light, the ever-changing images in the flames, the crackling sounds, the way in which you can become boiling hot on one side yet stay cold on the other, and the comfort of sitting by a fire when the weather outside is awful.

As the *flickering* group performed their piece to the rest of the class, another child spontaneously made a few *flickering* movements. Thus the music developed naturally into music/dance. First, the composers played their piece whilst another group moved. The dancers soon found that the piece moved between sections too fast for coherent movement to be possible. Next, the composers improvised around patterns from their piece whilst the dancers *flickered.* This improvisation took off. Individual musicians responded to the movement and to each other. The dancers responded to each other as well as to the music. Unfortunately this was not captured on video, and many ideas were forgotten. But the musicians and dancers together drew from what they remembered to draft a coherent piece of music/dance which gradually took on a more stable form.

The teacher found that the music about the comfort of sitting by a fire on a cheerless day made her think of another piece which was similarly inspired: the second movement of 'Winter' from Vivaldi's *The*

135

Four Seasons. In this piece, a smooth and song-like melody on the solo violin is accompanied quietly by throbbing cellos, with the first and second violins playing a fast, but even, pizzicato (plucked) figure. The viola part, which is very slow-moving and sustained, seems to glue the whole piece together. The line of poetry that Vivaldi wrote above this music suggests the quiet and content of someone sitting by the fire whilst it rains outside.[3] The teacher thinks of the solo violin line as representing a dreaming, solitary, listener. The pizzicato figure suggests the flickering of the flames (or is it the rain on the roof?) whilst the violas, cellos and bass provide warmth. She told the class about the line of poetry, and then played the piece. The composers commented thoughtfully about the similarities and differences of their piece and Vivaldi's. They thought that Vivaldi's use of sustaining instruments had enabled him to create a better feeling of warmth and content than they had. However, perhaps partly because they were so well inside their own piece, they thought that their less even use of gliding movements on a glockenspiel gave a more realistic impression of the firelight.

EXAMPLE TOPIC: *Growth*

The class had been reading and writing poems which 'grew'. Sarah, aged 8, used the plan of *This is the House that Jack Built* for her poem, *This is the Honey that Sarah Collected.* She wrote six verses. The first verse consisted of just one line. Subsequent verses consisted of the preceding verse with a new line added at the beginning. The class used Sarah's poem as the stimulus for a class composition. The longest verse had six lines, about the planting of seeds, the effect of the sun and rain, the opening of the flower, the collection of pollen by the bee, the departure of the bee to the hive, and Sarah's collection of honey from the hive. So the class divided into six groups, one to work on each line. Once the music had been devised, the teacher and class talked about the most effective way of organising the whole composition. They experimented with a variety of solutions:

1 *Sarah read the poem at a normal pace, and each line was accompanied by its music.*
   The children rejected this idea because their music was often only half complete when Sarah moved to a new line. The music was losing its sense.

2 *Sarah read each line at a normal pace, but paused between lines until the music had finished.*

136

The children did not like the way in which the verses were being chopped up. The poem was losing its sense.

3   *The music and poem were separated. Sarah read the first verse, and then the first verse was played. Sarah read the second verse, and then the second verse was played, one line after the other, and so on.*
    The children thought that this was an improvement, but wanted to organise the music so that it sounded less segmented.

4   *They kept the same basic structure: verse 1 (poem), verse 1 (music), verse 2 (poem), etc. But the music was restructured. Instead of each line stopping when the next one came in, it was repeated as necessary until the last line of the verse was complete. Thus the last musical line of the sixth verse consisted of six layers of music.*
    Now the children wanted to blur the edges between the spoken and played sections, and to decrease the length of the music, particularly for the later verses.

5   *They kept the same basic structure: verse 1 (poem), verse 1 (music), etc. But the music for verse 1 played, very quietly, throughout the composition. Musical lines did not wait for the previous one to be completed, but entered after a decent interval. Balance, and points of entry, were controlled by a conductor.*
    This was the final version.

Working between subjects

EXAMPLE TOPIC: *Our town*

The class visited their parish church. The atmosphere of the ancient stone-built structure with its vaulted roof, characteristic smell, and bright stained-glass windows contrasting sharply with the semi-darkness, made an impact on many of the children. Whilst they sat quietly in the pews, the organist had started to practise.

Once back at school, some children responded to the visit by writing and drawing. Another group decided to compose instead. Impressed by the low sounds of the organ, and the reverberation time of the church, the children chose instruments that produce low sustaining sounds: a bass xylophone, an electronic keyboard, and a cello. Their piece was slow, solemn and sustained.

EXAMPLE TOPIC: *Pattern*

Some children had been investigating the *Four-Colour Problem.*

After many hours of experiment, they gradually became convinced that, whatever pattern you draw, you never need more than four colours to arrange that no two areas with a common boundary are the same colour. They became interested in what they saw as the distinctiveness of the number *four*. They chose four xylophone notes – B(lue), C(herry), E(cru) and G(reen) – and started to assemble four-note melodies according to rules that they devised: adjacent notes must be different, and the melody must be interesting.

Music within the arts

Subdivision of the curriculum into areas such as science, the humanities, and so on, tends to result in music being placed in an area known under a variety of names including 'expressive arts' and 'creative arts'. I shall refer to this area simply as 'the arts'. The range of the arts curriculum is defined – by schools and others – in a number of ways. At its most narrow, it consists just of those National Curriculum foundation subjects (DES, 1989) which do not sit conveniently in any other area: music and visual art. A second definition includes also drama, dance, media, poetry, and other elements of the verbal arts. A definition that is broader still includes all the arts subjects, and the artistic parts of all other subjects. I have this final definition in mind as I write, though most of what I say applies particularly to the group of arts subjects that are usually taught in primary schools: music, visual art, drama and dance.

Thinking about the arts as a curriculum area, rather than as a set of discrete disciplines, makes sense because the arts have a number of shared concerns and values. They are concerned with aspects of aesthetic and cultural development which have value both within and beyond arts activity. As such, they form an essential component of a balanced education. They are not just optional extras to do with education for leisure, but are crucial to the development of the whole person. Grouping the arts means that those elements they have in common can be recognised, without loss of the individual arts' distinctive qualities. Thinking about music as part of arts education does not result in any compromise of musical standards or values, or in musical activity losing its individual identity. In particular, it does not mean the asphyxiation of music within some amorphous agglomeration of undistinguishable activities.

The arts curriculum can be organised in many ways. In some schools, the subjects operate independently of each other. In others, children work either between the arts – in an inter-arts mode – or in one art alone, as the need arises. In primary school, work between the arts can take place as a matter of course. A child who has made a painting uses it as a musical score. A composition may extend naturally into movement. Sybil Marshall's (1963) description of her village schoolchildren's use of Beethoven's *Pastoral Symphony* as a stimulus for movement, visual art, and writing gives a vivid example of how natural and fulfilling art unconstrained by subject boundary can be. In secondary school, inter-arts work has often been less easy because of specialist teaching and rigid timetabling. Thus pupils have missed out on opportunities to work between the arts, and to relate their work in one art to that in others. Grouping of arts teachers into a faculty structure, and rationalisation of timetabling, has resulted in the opportunities for flexible arts teaching – which have always existed in the primary school – occurring more frequently in secondary schools.

Moves towards the rationalisation of arts teaching have not been universally welcomed; many secondary schools still operate according to rigid subject divisions. Even where effective arts structures have been developed, this has often not been easy. Management has sometimes seen rationalisation as a way of saving timetable time and money, rather than the enrichment of artistic process. Some teachers have found difficulty in understanding the special time and resource requirements of arts disciplines other than their own. The changes have come too fast for those with little personal experience of working in any art other than their own specialism. Some of these difficulties have also been felt in primary schools.

Over the last decade or so, much has been learnt about the pros and cons of thinking about arts education, not just music education. *The Arts in Schools* (Calouste Gulbenkian Foundation, 1982) opened the debate in those schools that had yet to address the matter. The SCDC/NCC *Arts in Schools Project*, which ran for four years up to 1989, fuelled the debate as it provided practical support to schools trying to improve arts provision. There will never be total agreement about the role of music in the curriculum. Education would be exceedingly boring if everyone did always agree. But a consensus concerning the principles which must apply if arts education is to be artistic – and 'artistic' includes 'musical' – seems to be emerging.

1   **Arts education consists of a balance of two complementary activities: making and appraising[4]**
    Appraising, or 'understanding and becoming sensitive to the work of other people' (CGF, 1982: 40), helps children to make sense of

their culture. *Making* consists of observation, reflection and evaluation as well as doing. It is not just a matter of letting children express themselves:

> . . . expressive activity in the arts involves more than expressing whatever subjective state a person happens to be in at the time. Mere expression without reflection and evaluation need not lead to an understanding of the nature of personal feelings nor of the social values and acquired attitudes which influence them. It need carry people no nearer to understanding themselves.
>
> CGF, 1982: 40

This means that music, as an art, cannot be left to chance. One cannot just provide some materials and expect children to develop themselves through self-expression. Music education needs to be systematic without, of course, being constraining. We need to be prepared to teach skills and offer suggestions as appropriate, not just leave children to re-invent the wheel.

Ken Robinson (1989: 3) writes: 'It is now increasingly recognised that these [making and appraising] are equally important and related facets of arts education'. Traditionally, the balance between making and appraising in the individual arts has varied. In visual art, for instance, there has often been more focus on making than there has been in music. There is no reason why the balance of making and appraising should be exactly the same (whatever that means) in all the arts. But there has been some adjustment of balance within individual arts. Critical study of the work of visual artists is becoming more important. In general, music now involves more composing and proportionately less listening to the compositions of others.

2 **The arts are not interchangeable**
A child who is creative as a composer, for instance, will not necessarily be creative as a painter. Children who seem not to be creative in any field may just not have found any of the areas in which they can demonstrate their creativity. It follows that music has to be properly provided for. A dose of creativity in some other area is not sufficient. Learning to paint does not teach you how to sing; neither is it any substitute for it.

3 **Individual arts have differing requirements for timetabling**
Some activities are best developed in a sustained block of time. Others require opportunities for maturation between sessions.

140

Many aspects of music – singing for instance – work better in short bursts. Many visual arts activities, however, are best sustained for longer periods. In secondary schools, the different timetabling requirements of the individual arts can cause problems in the division of block timetables; in primary school there is much more freedom to timetable according to the need of the activity.

4 Arts education needs proper resourcing

High standards of achievement in the arts will be encouraged when children work . . . with media that enhance rather than inhibit their attempts at expression and communication.

CGF, 1982: 55

This means that children need a proper range and supply of instruments, beaters, and so on. Instruments wear out, and beaters get lost, and the music budget needs to reflect this.

The four points listed above could all relate to a model of arts education in which music took place as discrete activity. In fact, many of the activities mentioned already, both in this chapter and earlier, draw on other arts as well as music. Writing songs, composing in response to painting, and so on, all have the potential to be inter-arts, not just music-based, work. What turns writing songs, for instance, into inter-arts activity? To me, an activity becomes inter-arts when it is considered in terms of each of the arts it lies between. Writing a song becomes inter-arts when the lyrics are devised with the same attention and care that would be given to pure poetry – as well, of course, as the composition being considered musically. All the principles listed above apply also to inter-arts work. But there are some additional points to be considered:

1 Inter-arts work is about enrichment, not compromise

Inter-arts work can offer pupils a richer experience than they could receive through independently organised courses in the individual arts. This does not mean that pupils will necessarily spend any less time working in the individual arts. But this time will be utilised more effectively because pupils will be able to relate their individual art activity to the work they, and other pupils, are doing elsewhere in the arts. When pupils work in a coherent arts programme, rather than in independent individual arts, there is a sense in which the time they spend can be counted twice.

141

2   **In inter-arts work, individual art forms retain their artistic integrity**
Because inter-arts work is about enrichment, inter-arts music is still musical. A musical composition intended to accompany movement, for instance, is thought about just as carefully, and has the same musical validity, as a freestanding musical composition. Inter-arts work is not about the development of some hybrid form of combined arts, or of *combined artists* who have never thought about the extent to which they are painters, singers, or dancers.

3   **In inter-arts work, teachers can still use specialist expertise**
In secondary school, children may rotate round the arts, but their specialist teachers do not necessarily rotate with them. Music teachers working on arts programmes usually spend most of their time doing what they do best – music – though they are alert to the cross-arts implications of their work. Inter-arts work in primary school requires generalist teachers able to identify and respond to children's needs in all the arts. Ideally, teachers will also be practising artists in at least one art form – music, for instance. But it is not sensible to suggest that all primary teachers – or even those who have curriculum leadership responsibilities in the arts – can be practising artists in all fields: music, visual art, dance, and so on. Becoming a practising artist in just one field usually takes several years of progressive study and skill development. It is far better to have a visual artist with sensitivity across the arts than a Jack or Jill of all trades.

4   **Inter-arts work arises naturally in response to a stimulus**
There is no artistic purpose in contriving inter-arts work. Unfortunately, this has not always been well understood in initial teacher training, with the result that some student teachers enter the profession confused. I recall a proposal for an arts course for student teachers in which, over two years, students would move from working in individual art forms to, apparently, working in music, art and drama simultaneously. What for? It seems rather like asking someone to pat their head, rub their stomach, and jump up and down at the same time; a challenging feat of co-ordination with no discernible artistic value. Given any stimulus, some students may wish to respond in a mode that integrates music, art and drama, whilst others may prefer to use drama alone, for instance. Neither mode of response is necessarily *better* than the other. In particular, the students who choose a pure

142

drama response are not necessarily more narrow-minded, constrained, or immature than the others. Artists are free to move between artistic modes as they wish. Even Wagner, as he strove to produce his *gesamtkunstwerk* – a fusion of all the arts – chose to write pieces of pure music from time to time.

When student teachers – or children – are held back artistically through thinking of the individual arts only as discrete activities, then tutors and teachers need to step in and make suggestions about materials, or provide a stimulus which is amenable to an inter-arts response. What is objectionable is the notion that doing several things at once is necessarily better. It is just different.

Music within science

There is potential for music in any subject. Here, I take science as an example.

There are many phenomena which interest both musicians and scientists. For example:

o   Music exists as sound within time.
o   We hear music through our ears.
o   Music is dependent on materials, and the method by which they are played.
o   Our perception of music is determined by several factors, including our position relative to a sound source, and the acoustics of the environment.
o   Deaf people respond to music.
o   Guitar frets get closer together towards the bridge because of the roughly logarithmic relationship between pitch and frequency.
o   Our perception of high notes deteriorates with age, and after visits to discos.
o   Horn-players who sit at the back of an orchestra find that they need to make a conscious effort to play ahead of the beat that they hear from the first violins.
o   We can predict the fundamental note of a tuba by measuring its vibrating length, and then measure the error of our prediction using our ears.
o   We can predict where a violin string should be stopped to produce a particular harmonic, and then account for inaccuracy in terms of the inflexibility of strings.

o We can use computer software to synthesise an oboe tone, harmonic by harmonic.

All these topics can be taught in a mode which is musical as well as scientific. But I shall focus on a narrow area of commonality between science and music in the primary curriculum. In the table on pages 146–147, I give the part of the Programmes of Study for Attainment Target 4 for science in the National Curriculum (DFE, 1995) which relates to sound, and makes suggestions about how the scientific content might be developed or reinforced musically. Many of my suggestions are for listening, often in combination with looking. Most suggestions amount to little more than encouraging children to observe the effects of their investigations with their ears as well as their eyes. Listening could, of course, lead to performing and composing whenever the teacher wished. My suggestions tie in with the music National Curriculum, and also with the objectives set for 7- and 11-year-olds in *Music from 5 to 16* (DES, 1985a).

Many of my suggestions for music are very similar to those in Part One; the music that overlaps with science is not special music. Very few of my musical suggestions are not scientific too. Attainment Target 4 is a powerful illustration of how working between subjects can save time. It cannot, on its own, provide a music education which is systematic or adequate. One could not hope to teach music by only teaching science. But musical interpretation of the Programme of Study can mean that children reinforce their scientific learning, and arrive at music sessions better prepared. Activity in music really can stimulate, and be stimulated by, activity in science. And, of course, the same is true for other pairs of subjects.

Music as a learning medium

There are many situations in which music may be used as a learning medium, not just as an end in itself. Counting songs can be used to reinforce number concepts. In music therapy, music is used as a means of communication between therapist and client. I shall take just one particular example: the promotion of language development through music. As language and music are both concerned with sound, they have some common basis. I shall outline two psychological studies which look at language development and music from different angles. The first, by Audrey Wisbey, concerns the relationship between childhood hearing loss and difficulties with language development. The second, by Peter Bryant and Lynette Bradley, considers the relationship between the ability to rhyme and alliterate and reading development. Though Bryant and Bradley write about sound awareness in a general, not just musical, sense, their work has implications for music education.

Audrey Wisbey's theories received extensive media coverage in the early 1980s. Whilst a teacher, Wisbey became concerned by the number of apparently intelligent children who fail to become literate. In *Music as the Source of Learning* (Wisbey, 1980), she attributes the literacy difficulties of many children to hearing problems including common ailments such as catarrh, sinusitis and infected tonsils in early childhood. Even when children's residual hearing is assessed as 'within the limits of normality', there can be serious hearing loss of high-frequency sounds. This can result, Wisbey believes, in insufficient or inaccurate learning of speech sounds. By the time that the cause of the hearing problem is diagnosed and attended to, the child will have lost some high-frequency hearing through ageing; thus it can be too late for pre-literacy auditory learning to take place. The relationship between hearing and language learning is probably two-way; Leontiev (1969) attributed the superior pitch discrimination ability of some Vietnamese people to the tonal nature of their language. Unlike people whose language is less tonal, their pitch discrimination did not deteriorate when tones were presented using the usually difficult 'u' and 'e' sounds instead of pure tones.

Wisbey emphasises the importance of early music education. It facilitates the identification of hearing problems, and reinforces learning of the sounds that form the components of speech. Her approach to music education is controlled, systematic and progressive. Children work with the raw ingredients of music – pitch, duration, intensity, timbre, rhythm, and so on – and learn simple sounds before moving on to more complex ones. I would quibble with some details of her method. In *Learn to Sing to Learn to Read* (Wisbey, 1981), for instance, the simple to complex progression is applied even to the number of notes that children use. For some weeks, the children use only middle C. This would seem to me to be potentially boring, and difficult to justify as neither music nor language requires the ability to recall or identify precise pitches, sometimes known as absolute pitch or perfect pitch. But many of the activities, which include careful listening often combined with spatial awareness, are very valuable. Many are similar to those suggested in the section on music within science. The important

145

Science programmes of study	Suggestions for music

KEY STAGE 1 Reception–Year 2

Pupils should be taught:
- that there are many kinds of sounds and many sources of sound;
- that sound travels away from sources, getting fainter as they do so;
- that sounds are heard when they enter the ear.

1 Close listening to sounds (e.g. 'Sit quietly for a minute ... What did you hear? ... Did everyone hear Ross move his foot? ... Why not?')
2 Describing sounds (e.g. 'How is Mark's sound different from Julie's sound? . . . Yes, it is faster . . . Claire said it was brighter, too. Claire, can you find me a sound which is brighter still?').
3 Identifying sounds of which the sources are hidden (e.g. 'What is the noise we can hear from outside? . . . Is it a car or a motorbike?' or 'Peter is sitting round the corner with some instruments. When he starts to play one, I'd like you to pick the same instrument from this set here and copy him.')
4 Experimenting on improvised and purchased instruments.
5 Composing using resources defined according to the method of sound production (e.g. 'Here are some different types of elastic bands, and some boxes of different sizes. See how many different plucked sounds you can make . . . Tony played us a melody on his bands . . . What other melodies can you make?').
6 Investigating the effect of playing instruments in unconventional ways (e.g. blowing into the holes of a guiro).
7 Making cassette recordings of sounds made in various ways for other children to identify.

The Programmes of Study for Attainment Target 4 (physical processes) for science in the National Curriculum are set out in full in the Department for Education document *The National Curriculum (England)* (1995) HMSO, London.

Science programmes of study	Suggestions for music

KEY STAGE 2   Year 3–Year 6

Pupils should be taught:

- that sounds are made when objects, eg *strings on musical instruments*, vibrate but that vibrations are not always directly visible;
- that the pitch and loudness of sounds produced by some vibrating objects, eg *a drum skin, a plucked string*, can be changed;
- that vibrations from sound sources can travel through a variety of materials, *eg metals, wood, glass, air*, to the ear.

1 Further experimenting with improvised and purchased instruments.
2 Further investigation of how instruments work.
3 Experimenting and performing on *stringed instruments*:
  - Noticing which end of a stopped string vibrates, visually and by touch.
  - Hearing the effect of damping a vibrating string.
  - Investigating the relationship between pitch and vibrating length.
  - Noting that lower strings are thicker.
  - Investigating the effect of tension on the pitch of a plucked elastic band.
  - Feeling the vibration in the sound box of a guitar.
  - Considering the differing duration of plucked and bowed strings.

  And so on.
4 Experimenting and performing on *wind instruments*:
  - Noting that lower instruments are typically larger.
  - Tuning a set of milk bottles to give a melody when blown across by adjusting the amount of water they contain.
  - Listening to the effect of embouchure on the precise pitch of a milk-bottle note.
  - Blowing and overblowing recorders.

  And so on.
5 Experimenting and performing on *percussion instruments*:
  - Choosing beaters to give a particular effect.
  - Listening to the unevenness caused when using an unmatched pair of beaters.
  - Noticing that drums and so on do have a pitch and that the pitch of drums sometimes depends on how and where they are hit.
  - Observing the inside of a piano: the effects of the pedals, hammers and dampers, the gradation of string length and thickness, duplication and triplication of strings.

  And so on.

147

difference is that Wisbey believes these activities should commence in early childhood – long before the child reaches Key Stage 2.

In *Children's Reading Problems*, Peter Bryant and Lynette Bradley (1985) report their findings that backward readers are often very poor at detecting rhyme and alliteration. In particular, children who are poor rhymers at the age of 4 or 5 tend to be poorer readers and spellers at the age of 8 or 9. This result is independent of the tested intelligence of the children concerned. This led Bryant and Bradley to pose two questions. Can children be taught to rhyme and alliterate? If so, does this, on its own, improve their reading? The answer to both questions was 'yes'. Sixty-five children aged 6 were divided into four groups. During forty sessions over two years, Group 1 was taught about rhyme and alliteration. Within the same time allocation, Group 2 was taught also to relate rhyme and alliteration to their reading. Group 3 was a taught control group; the members attended forty special sessions over two years, but were taught material other than rhyme and alliteration. Group 4 was a control group which had no special experimental tuition. At the end of the two-year period, the children in Group 2 were found, allowing for other factors, to have a reading age that was six months greater than Group 1, ten months greater than Group 3, and fourteen months greater than Group 4. Thus learning to rhyme and alliterate improved reading, but the greater improvement occurred when the rhyming and alliteration were applied specifically to reading.

Rhyming and alliteration can be developed in many ways. Bryant and Bradley used pictures of named objects. Drawing attention to rhyme in the lyrics of songs, including nursery rhymes, could help with language development.

The work of Bryant and Bradley, and that of Wisbey, indicates the use of music as a learning medium in language development. This is constructive for music as well as language: when the singing of rhymes, and learning about the parameters of music, is handled musically, then musical development is taking place at the same time as language development. But consideration of these studies reminds us – if we ever needed to be reminded – that we cannot organise the curriculum for any subject – be it music, language or science – simply by relying on experience in other subject areas. According to Wisbey, it seems that the music included in Key Stage 2 for science will take place too late for it to be of much value in promoting children's verbal literacy. Bryant and Bradley's findings that the best gains in reading ability were

148

obtained when rhyming and alliteration *were applied to reading* indicate that singing nursery rhymes, alone, will not maximise the potential of rhyme to increase children's reading ability. Cross-curriculum work offers marvellous opportunities for counting time at least twice. But subject-specific development cannot take place through haphazard encounter in other subject areas. Musical development through music-language, music-science or music-anything requires specific musical relevance.

Music within the primary school

'Taking up an instrument seriously is like a life sentence.'
Ronnie Scott, *Observer Sayings of the Week*, 5 August 1984

Up to now, we have focused on music within the common curriculum of primary children. In a sense, we have shut the classroom door, and ignored the world outside. In fact, curriculum music is often not the only music taking place in primary school. Many schools also offer additional activities for some children. These activities may take place outside class time, and may involve additional teachers, perhaps instrument teachers, or secondary music teachers. How can we see both class music and additional musical activities as operating within a coherent policy for school music? I start by reviewing my guidelines for primary music.

School music

In chapter 1, I wrote of music in primary school as:

o   an active subject consisting of the interdependent activities of listening, performing and composing
o   for all pupils and all teachers
o   valuable only if enjoyable.

Hitherto, we have developed these ideas through thinking about music in classrooms. But how do voluntary additional activities, such as choirs drawn from several classes, fit in? In general, the additional activities operate within these guidelines. The activities are concerned with composing, performing or listening. They are open to all pupils and teachers. Observation of the children shows that they are enjoying themselves. But is there a coherent relationship between the class music and the additional activities? In some schools, the class music and extra activities are well integrated and mutually supporting. The voluntary activities – choirs, orchestras, instrument lessons and so on – enrich classroom music by enabling children to extend themselves according to individual interest and need. Children who particularly enjoy singing are able to do more than is possible during class time by joining a choir. Those ready to read music before their peers, can learn to play the recorder from notation. Those ready to learn an orchestral instrument are given the opportunity to do so. But although these activities take place at different times from classroom music, they do not take place independently. Instrumentalists bring their instruments into the classroom and use them during composing and performing activities. Their performance provides the stimulus for listening activity, and often results in more children wanting to take up instruments. The choir members' enthusiasm for singing becomes a catalyst for increased singing development in the class as a whole.

These extra activities are sometimes referred to as *extra-curricular*. This can give the impression that they are separate from the class music curriculum, rather than an extension of it. So here I refer to them as *extension music*.

In some schools, the classroom music and the extra activities are less well integrated. Two separate systems operate. All children receive classroom music, and some also participate in other activities. In some cases admission to extra-curricular groups is by interest, and in others children are selected. This is extra-curricular music in the most narrow sense of the term – music that literally lies outside the music curriculum. The independent operation of curricular and extra-curricular music, combined with the relatively high public profile that extra-curricular groups often have, can lead children, teachers, and parents to believe that extra-curricular music is more important. A school music policy that values extra-curricular music above cur-riculum music is harmful. First, it is divisive: not all children participate in the higher-status activity. Children become divided into two groups, one of which is often termed 'musical', so that the other one comes to regard itself as 'unmusical'. Thus children view themselves as hopeless in music long before they have started to think about their ability in other subjects. Second, it can lead to curriculum music becoming less coherent. Teachers worn out by a high-priority series of extra-curricular activities may cut corners when it comes to curriculum music. Class music may be organised haphazardly and without attention to individual needs or progression; indeed, it may consist almost entirely of massed sing-songs or radio and TV programmes. Communal singing is fun as a treat, but it is not an efficient way of developing the singing of the children who most need help, or stretching the more able. Radio and TV programmes can be a valuable

151

resource for teachers to work round, but are never a replacement for a music curriculum designed to take account of individual differences and needs. Would teachers devolve responsibility for their entire mathematics curriculum to the BBC?

There is no purpose in thinking about curricular and extra-curricular music separately. There is no voluntary activity that cannot take place, or standard that cannot be reached, within a model of school music in which curriculum music, the focus of activity, is enriched by extension music. Thinking about school music as a coherent whole ensures that all children receive the planned music education to which they are entitled.

Extension music

Extension music, then, consists of music activities that are additional to those participated in by the whole class. The instrument lessons often provided by visiting specialists are a component to which we turn later. Here, I focus on the extension activities led by school teachers. Of what might these consist? This depends on the interests and expertise of the contributing staff and the children. Choirs, recorder groups and orchestras are common. Some schools are resourced for pop groups and steel bands. In others, children and teachers meet regularly at lunchtimes to explore the links between music and dance, or to work with music computer software. The possibilities are limitless. The important point is that the extension music extends what is already going on in classrooms; it is not an alternative system.

Two questions about the organisation of activities arise:

1   Should membership be open or selected?
2   Should casual attendance be permitted?

The answers to these questions depend on the nature of the activity. An instrumental group rehearsing systematically and progressively over several weeks for a performance requires consistent membership, but an instrumental group that meets weekly for one-off sessions does not. Membership may have to be restricted if there are not enough resources, such as synthesisers, to go round. Some activities may be designed with a particular group of children in mind, for instance some unusually advanced recorder players. But many activities can take place with open membership and casual attendance. In many schools, this mode of operation is the norm, with other modes being regarded as exceptions which need to be justified.

In the past, it was common for the members of choirs, for instance, to be selected. The membership of the choir at the junior school I attended was determined by a sort of compulsory audition. All children – whether we were interested in joining the choir or not – sang individually to our teacher in front of the rest of the class. As we had never sung solos in school before, many of us felt fairly foolish. At least we were not left in suspense as to the outcome of the audition. As soon as a solo was over, the soloist was directed to stand in one of two lines: the *passes* and the *fails*. Choir members had badges presented to them in assembly. We were told that the word *choir* was written in silver, not gold, lettering, as a mark of the light, silvery, quality of our voices. Brassy voices were out. I still have my badge somewhere, along with the *attendance* badge which I gained through being blessed with such good health that I had not been ill for an entire year.

The school choir met weekly to rehearse songs which we sang in non-competitive festivals. During daily assembly, we sat smugly on benches at the front, facing the children with brassy voices who were seated cross-legged on the floor. We marched out of the hall ahead of them. I enjoyed my time in the choir. Doubtless, I learnt a lot from it. But what good came from leaving out other children? Would they develop silvery voices by being given less opportunity to sing? Did the odd brassy voice matter, if we were not competing for anything? And were they all left unscarred by the daily reminder of their musical inferiority?

I left primary school in 1965, a time when competition was more a part of primary school life than it is now. Set in the context of 11-plus examinations, streaming from the age of 7, termly form placings, and the dreaded annual sports days in which incompetents like myself had no option but to make public fools of themselves (whilst 'letting down' the blue team . . .), there was nothing particularly evil about the way in which the choir was organised. But whereas the 11-plus has all but disappeared, and sports days have become quite jolly affairs, here and there the selected choir still survives. I have visited a primary classroom where the sole list of children's names on the wall announces who has been selected by audition for the choir. Jonathan, aged 8, is not on the list. I asked him about his favourite songs. 'I am no good at singing,' he said.

My argument for regarding open membership as the norm is to do with decreasing the number of children who label themselves as unmusical, and reducing the sort of competition that is futile. My case

153

for regarding the possibility of casual attendance as the norm is different; primary age children are often not in a position to understand the musical and educational reasons for committed attendance. It is agreed that the progress of musical ensembles is usually greater when the total membership is present for every rehearsal. Ensemble playing is not just a matter of getting your notes right. An ensemble is not just a group of individuals whose playing is synchronised by a human starting-pistol sometimes known as a conductor. Ideally, an ensemble sounds and feels like a single composite instrument. This has to be practised; hence the advantage of consistent membership. The problem is that it is difficult for anyone to understand this if they have not been in an ensemble that has at least started to achieve the composite instrument feeling. Many younger primary children have not. If we do not let them join in some activities on a casual basis, at least to begin with, they may not come at all. That way, they will never come to appreciate the musical reasons for sustained attendance. And, more importantly, they will never have the experience of participating in ensemble performance.

Instrument teaching

What part can the instrument specialists who visit some schools play in school music? In some LEAs, the specialists have been absorbed into Music Support Services which perform a number of functions, often including supporting the work of primary class teachers. Here, the work of the school and the visiting teacher is already well integrated. This section is concerned particularly with the more traditional arrangement in which instrument teachers visit schools with the explicit purpose of teaching groups, and possibly individuals, to play instruments. Over the last few years, the range of instruments taught in many regions has expanded to include instruments of non-Western cultures and pop music instruments. The examples in this section refer to systems in which teaching is almost exclusively confined to orchestral and band instruments. However, some of the points I make have wider applicability.

Instrument teaching sometimes operates completely independently of class teaching. The instrument teacher visits the school, gives lessons out of earshot, and then disappears into the distance. The only evidence of his or her presence is the periodic purposeful movement round the school of groups of children carrying violin cases.

This can be a great waste of an expensive resource. Children's musical development can become divided into two compartments – school music and instrument lessons – which may have little in common, or may overlap without purpose. The school as a whole does not gain from the presence of the instrument teachers.

Instrument lessons can be regarded as a form of extension music; an optional activity for children interested in developing as performers. Usually, instrument teachers welcome opportunities to meet with members of a school's music staff to plan this. Travelling round a series of schools all day, with little contact with adults, and little sustained contact with anyone, is a lonely business which can feel aimless. Links between instrument lessons and school music can commence with including instrument teachers in the discussion of school music policy and, where their terms of employment permit this, inviting instrument teachers to spend part of their time in school working with classes, or with extension activities such as orchestras. This can often lead to effective and early integration of instrumentalists into class music and other extension activities.

Instrument lessons, even when available without charge, often need to be made exceptions to the norms of casual attendance and open membership. If children do not attend lessons regularly, they are unlikely to make sustained progress. It would be difficult for instrument teachers, who are usually only in each school for a few hours each week, to build sufficient flexibility into their teaching to be able to accommodate ever-changing groups. Many schools seek parental support for sustained attendance before tuition commences. But children cannot be expected to understand the musical reasons for this if they have not had some previous experience of learning to play an instrument. Thus the option of instrument lessons is best preceded by opportunities to participate in activities organised on a more casual basis. Even with the very best of preparation, it is inevitable that some children will still want to give up lessons within a few weeks of starting. It is very difficult to know whether you are going to like playing the flute until you have tried it. And no matter how carefully you explain to children that it will be many years before they become accomplished flautists, some will still be bitterly disappointed when they are unable to emulate the performance of James Galway within three or four weeks. Whilst encouraging children to regard instrument lessons as a commitment, we need to accept that some children will still want to give up. And overstressing the seriousness of taking up instrument lessons is not always in children's best interests. An example serves as an illustration:

> Ann took up the violin in response to a fortunate second offer of lessons in school at the age of 12. Her first chance had been three years earlier. Interested children had been told to think seriously about whether they could guarantee that they would not want to give up. If so, they should tell their teacher. Ann obeyed these instructions to the letter. She thought seriously, realised that she could not guarantee that she would never want to give up, and so did not tell her teacher anything. Most of the 9-year-olds who took up the violin gave up within a term or so. Ann is now a successful violin teacher.

Ideally, instrument lessons would be open to everyone who wanted them. In fact, the supply of instruments and lesson time is often insufficient to cope with demand. Thus, selection for instrument lessons becomes inevitable. On what basis should it be made? This depends on the purpose of the instrument lessons. Are they intended to enrich the education of gifted musicians, such as those who will eventually become professional performers? If so, we need some sort of predictive test of musical ability. Or are they part of the musical extension offered optionally to all children? If so, then we want to find the children who will get the greatest benefit (whatever we mean by this) from their lessons. In fact, these two views of the purpose of instrument lessons are not as incompatible as they might at first seem. The children who will become the professional performers of tomorrow are amongst those who will benefit from instrument lessons. Thus a selection system that aims to identify children who will most profit from lessons – musically, educationally, and socially – will, if it is successful, result in so-called gifted children, amongst a lot of other children, starting lessons.

Before deciding how to devise a system, it is useful to reflect on how we will measure its effectiveness. In the past, this has sometimes been assessed in terms of the proportion of children who continue lessons for sustained periods. Or rather, to be more accurate, ineffectiveness has been assessed in terms of the proportion of children giving up. Mawbey (1973) writes of 'the problem of wastage from instrumental classes', and attributes it to selection procedures which are insufficiently rigorous in, for instance, 'screening out those who have no musical talent'. The idea that an effective selection system is one in which there is little, or preferably no, drop-out has been implicit in more recent investigations (for example, Cooper, 1985).

I do not accept that a child who gives up instrument lessons necessarily forms evidence of the failure of a selection procedure. In fact, I have difficulty with the idea that effectiveness is about how long children continue with lessons, or the ultimate level of their performance. How long do children have to carry on before we judge them successes? Is a child who persists with violin tuition until she leaves school and then never touches a violin again a success? Is another who only takes flute lessons for two terms but then buys himself an electric guitar and forms a pop group a failure? How good do children have to get before we judge them successes? Do they have to be accepted into music college, or is a more modest performance level, perhaps Grade Five of the examinations conducted by the Associated Board of the Royal Schools of Music, enough? If the former, then the success rate must be embarrassingly small in every LEA throughout the country. If the latter, then we still have a problem: to what extent can Grade Five, for instance, be judged a mark of musical achievement? Grade Five performers will still find most of the standard classical repertoire played by even the humblest local amateur orchestra well beyond their reach. The effectiveness of selection cannot be measured solely in terms of performing attainment or staying power. Children who end up accomplished performers *are* successes; but then so are those who have benefited in any other way from their lessons. These include children who have grown in confidence, or social skills, as well as those who have learnt the most modest of music skills which could act as the foundation for others in the future. This leads to measures of selection effectiveness which are more woolly than continuation rates or attainment levels. It means that we need to think of effectiveness in terms of what individuals have learnt, in the widest sense, through their lessons. But this is something which we have to accept if we think that instrument teaching is about extension for everyone, not just enrichment for the jet set. Perhaps new initiatives in educational assessment, such as Records of Achievement, will help us to involve pupils in their own assessment of what they have learnt from instrument lessons.

I have suggested the following:

1   Instrument teaching should be available to those children who will benefit from it. This includes those whose ultimate musical achievement will be modest, as well as those who will eventually become highly accomplished musicians.

2   Likely perseverance in instrument lessons is a quality to be valued. But it is not the be-all and end-all of successful selection.

3   Children who give up tuition have not necessarily wasted their places.

That said, it makes sense to organise instrument teaching so that children are encouraged to continue with tuition, and make as much progress as possible. One of the ways of doing this is to give some consideration to whether individuals might be particularly suited to one instrument rather than another. The allocation of children to instruments is sometimes a little haphazard.

So how might selection be organised? We want a system that selects persevering potential high-flyers, but does not screen out other keen pupils. We want children to end up playing the instruments on which they will make the most progress. There is no perfect way of organising selection for anything. We just have to try to decrease the number of mistakes we make. And there is no ideal system of selecting children for instrument lessons which can be applied in all situations; those responsible have to decide how best to operate in their particular circumstances. But there are some steps which teachers can take to increase the validity of the criteria that they use when selecting, and, most importantly, children use when choosing.

1   Allow children to become familiar with several instruments before choosing one

Surprising though it may seem, some children arrive at their first instrument lesson without knowing what their chosen instrument either looks or sounds like. This cannot increase their chance of success. Suppose they do not like the sound? Suppose there is another instrument which makes a sound that they would prefer to make? Suppose there is no room for the cello on the minibus on which they travel to school each day?

Before choosing an instrument, children can become familiar with the sound and sight of several. Ideally, this will be through high-quality live performances, perhaps by teachers, concert performers, parents, secondary pupils, or primary pupils. Groups should be small enough for children to be close to the instrument, and have a chance to ask questions. Recordings combined with pictures are a poor alternative to live performance.

2 Do not place too much weight on whether a child can initially make a pleasant sound on an instrument

Instrument teachers faced with the problem of selecting a few children from a large number who want lessons sometimes resort to passing an instrument round, and seeing who can make the best sound. This is successful selection in the sense that the number of children left is reduced, but a correlation between an initial ability to play an instrument and ultimate achievement, for instance, is unproven. In fact, one can find many counter-examples – professional horn players who spent their first three lessons unable to produce a note, for example. Children can be taught to blow wind and brass instruments; those who can do so initially simply have a head start, and will be easier for the teacher to teach in the first instance. Consequently, if children are permitted to try to play instruments as part of the familiarisation stage suggested above, those who produce only weird sounds, or even no sounds at all, should be reminded that tuition could help to remedy this.

3 Beware of physical suitability, personality, and gender stereotypes

There is a mythology associated with the gender, personality, and physical attributes which make children suitable, or unsuitable, to play particular instruments. Like most mythology, some of it has been around for a long time. As long ago as 1935, two Americans, Charles Lamp and Noel Keys (1935), were prompted to investigate some supposed correlations between physical attributes and instrumental achievement. Teachers told the researchers that lip-thickness is relevant to pupils' most appropriate choice of brass instrument: pupils should choose instruments with a mouthpiece size corresponding to the thickness of their lips. Thus thin-lipped pupils should choose instruments such as horns and trumpets, whilst those with thick lips should choose instruments such as trombones and tubas. This view is presumably based on the notion that thick lips will vibrate better at the lower frequencies, i.e. lower notes, played by trombones and tubas. Teachers also told Lamp and Keys that string players need long fingers, and wind players need even teeth. Subsequent investigation of the relationship between children's progress on instruments, and their possession of supposedly advantageous physical attributes, did not confirm these hypotheses.[1] Indeed the boy with the thinnest lips, and the boy with the thickest lips, both went on to become proficient French horn players. Sixty years later, we still sometimes find physical characteristics such as these being used to select pupils for instruments. Early in the 1980s (Mills, 1983) I interviewed fifty instrument teachers to find out what physical attributes each thought predicted success on the instruments on which they gave lessons. I found that some of the assumptions held by the teachers in Lamp and Keys' investigation are still commonly held. In addition, teachers explained why they believe that some other physical attributes are important. For instance, some bassoon teachers believe that bassoonists need particularly even front teeth because of the way in which the bassoon double reed is held. Some percussion teachers believe that percussionists need particularly fine motor co-ordination because of the high control of fine movement required during the performance of intricate rhythms. A handful of teachers declined to teach pupils who had supposedly undesirable physical attributes. But amongst other teachers' pupils I found high-flying instrumentalists with all sorts of supposedly undesirable features: short-armed trombonists, thick-lipped trumpeters, left-handed cellists, thin-lipped oboists, buck-teethed bassoonists, clumsy percussionists, and so on. As in selection by passing an instrument round, selection by physical attribute achieves the desired purpose of reducing the number of children present, but it has little to do with selection of children with high potential for achievement.

I have found (Mills, 1988b) a physical characteristic that predicts instrumental achievement better than any of the criteria which the teachers were using: left hand digital formula. To assess yours, place your left hand palm down on a flat surface, with your fingers together. Note whether your index finger or your ring finger reaches further up your middle finger. If your ring finger reaches further you have an $I < R$ formula, along with about 70% of the general population. Otherwise, you have the less usual $I > R$ formula (see Figure 8). I compared the left hand digital formula of some accomplished in-strumentalists[2] with that of a general population. Hardly any of the violin or viola players had the $I > R$ formula. Yet a majority of the other performers had the unusual $I > R$ formula.

Digital formula is not customarily used in any type of musical selection. I came across it in an anatomy textbook (Jones, 1941), not a music textbook. It is reasonable to suppose that the distribution of digital formula in children starting lessons on any instrument will be much the same as in the general population. It seems, though, that digital formula is predisposing some children towards success: the $I < R$ formula benefits violinists and viola players, and the $I > R$ formula

160

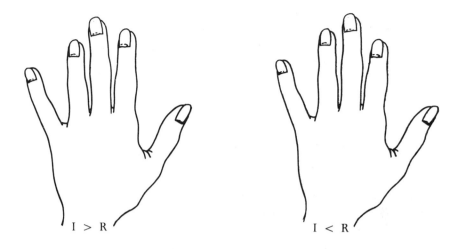

Figure 8   Left hand digital formula.

promotes success on other orchestral instruments. Yet it would be preposterous to suggest that digital formula should become part of any selection procedure, for two main reasons:

○   We do not know whether the apparent relationship between formula and success is inevitable, or the result of insensitive teaching. Think, for instance, of the left-hand positions which violinists of differing digital formula must adopt in order to rest all their left-hand fingertips on a string simultaneously. Much string technique is learnt by copying a teacher. If the teacher has an I < R formula, but has not noticed that a student has an I > R formula, is copying likely to result in the student developing a useful left-hand technique?

○   Some people without the preferred formula are succeeding. So even if the general association between formula and success is nothing to do with teaching, screening according to digital formula would result in some potential professional musicians being denied lessons.

There is just one occasion on which the physical attributes of normal children might render them unsuitable to start some instruments: when they are insufficiently physically mature, that is, still too small. A child may have too small a hand-span to be able to stretch between the keys on a clarinet, for instance. But these occasions are infrequent. Violins and cellos can be obtained in a variety of sizes to suit children

161

from the age of around 3 onwards. Violins can be used as small violas, and cellos can be strung as small double basses. A trombonist just unable to reach the lowest, seventh, position can avoid using it until she or he has grown a little. Flutes with U-shaped tubes, suitable for children not able to reach the full length of a standard flute, are occasionally seen.

Decisions that a child cannot start an instrument because of small size are only temporary; children do eventually grow. All standard instruments are suitable for large and small adults. Neville Marriner may, or may not, have been serious when he said that 'only really very tall conductors can deal adequately with slow music'. But orchestras include large piccolo players and small double-bass players who demonstrate a formidable technique in fast music, slow music, and that which lies between.

We have seen the dangers in over-generalising findings that the majority of successful performers of any instrument have particular physical attributes. The same is true for attributes of personality. Although the personality structure of musicians has been investigated in a serious and sustained manner (Kemp, 1981), potential pupils may occasionally be allocated to instruments on the basis of evidence scarcely above the level of the following orchestral clarinetist's summary of the orchestra: 'the brass are drinkers, the wind are thinkers, and the strings are stinkers' (Davies, 1978: 203). Personality stereotyping abounds in music. The social structure of orchestras seems to reinforce it. But it has yet to be proved that any measured difference in the personality of different categories of successful instrumentalists is present at the start of tuition, rather than arising during it, perhaps through contact with the stereotyping.

In *The Right Instrument for Your Child*, Atarah Ben-Tovim and Douglas Boyd (1985) describe an instrument selection system that is intended to help parents choose the instrument to which their child is best suited. This system includes personality assessment – parents assess whether the personality of their child matches that of some successful young performers whom Ben-Tovim and Boyd have observed. Again, we see unjustified generalisation of attributes. If Ben-Tovim and Boyd have observed that most successful young horn players 'prefer to relate to small groups and usually have just one or two close friends', should we really steer particularly popular children towards another instrument? Ben-Tovim and Boyd's statements about personality suitability seem closely related to the role of the instrument concerned in the symphony orchestra. For instance, in the symphony orchestra, large numbers of first and second violins play the same part. Thus it might be thought that violinists need sheep-like characteristics. And, Ben-Tovim and Boyd do indeed tell us that the violin is suitable for 'quietly behaved children' with 'no outlet for boisterousness or exuberance'. Orchestral trumpeters have their own, frequently prominent, part. Thus, Ben-Tovim and Boyd tell us that the trumpet is suitable for the 'individualist' with 'prima donna temperament'. The list continues. Symphony orchestras include plenty of extrovert violinists who are not in the throes of a personality crisis. One of the attributes of all successful violinists must surely be that they like some of the sounds made by violins. Yet children's preference amongst instrument sounds forms no part of Ben-Tovim and Boyd's method. In fact, the child does not seem to be in on the choice at all.

There is no evidence that children of either gender are predisposed towards success on any instrument. Yet it is common knowledge that some instruments are considered – by parents and children – to be more suitable for boys than girls, and vice versa. Girls tend to choose small, high-pitched orchestral instruments, boys tend to choose the large, low-pitched ones. There is no practical reason for this.[3] Girls are, clearly, capable of carrying and holding large instruments. Indeed, at the age at which tuition usually starts, around 11, girls are often bigger and stronger than boys. And as boys usually start instrument tuition before their voices break, they cannot be choosing low-pitched instruments because of a correspondence with their own vocal range.[4]

The association of gender with instruments is not just a British problem. Harold Abeles and Susan Porter (1978) found, in the USA, that parents' choice of instruments for sons differed from that for daughters. Adults were given eight instruments to choose from. Clarinets, flutes and violins were preferred for daughters, whilst drums, trombones and trumpets were preferred for sons, and the cello and saxophone were without significant gender association. The children's personal preferences for the instruments of the appropriate gender association were developing by the age of 7, and stable by the age of 9. Philip Griswold and Denise Chroback (1981) replicated much of this investigation. Their experimental evidence added harps, piccolos, glockenspiels, cellos, pianos, French horns, and oboes to the feminine list, and guitars, cymbals, saxophones, double basses and tubas to the masculine list.

Gender stereotyping is to be deplored because it decreases the choice of instruments available to both boys and girls. What can we do

163

to help remove it, or at least avoid reinforcing it? The last stage of Abeles and Porter's investigation provides a clue. They investigated the effect on children's gender associations of different methods of presenting the instruments and found, not surprisingly, that photographs of girls playing 'feminine' instruments and boys playing 'masculine' instruments were part of the problem, particularly for boys. So it seems likely that we could reduce the gender association of instruments through positive presentation of performers of the 'wrong' sex for their instrument. Take a look at the music books in your class library, and the music posters on your classroom walls, and consider removing any that reinforce stereotypes. But do not go over the top. The odd holiday postcard from Wales displaying a woman with a large black hat playing a harp will not, I think, do lasting harm to children. And I would not recommend following Abeles and Porter's findings concerning boys' particular susceptibility to pictorial gender associations to a logical conclusion of presenting pictures of males playing everything. I recall a children's book in which males play all the orchestral instruments, whilst the females are confined to blowing across bottles, and playing plastic recorders. This does not do much for the professional aspirations of female musicians.

As a teacher in a comprehensive school in the heart of brass band land, I found that whilst roughly even numbers of girls and boys were interested in playing the cornet and trumpet, no girls wanted to take up the trombone. I attempted to resolve this through role modelling: I took up the trombone myself. The scale of the gender bias concerning trombones in this locality became apparent when I made my debut at a school concert. As I walked onto the platform carrying a trombone, a portion of the audience dissolved into laughter, and that was before I played anything. My subsequent rendition of a bass line to *Raindrops Keep Falling on My Head* was, not surprisingly, insufficient to remove gender stereotyping overnight. But female trumpeters started to take my trombone away for a bit of surreptitious lunchtime practice. It did seem that role modelling was helpful, even at this late, secondary, age.

4   Consider apparent motivation, but do not over-rate it

We would probably all agree that a child will not receive much benefit from instrument lessons unless she or he is motivated to want to play the instrument. The problem is that motivation can be ill-informed. A child over the moon about the prospect of cello lessons may not have understood – however many times you have told him – that learning to play any instrument is a slow business. A child who has understood this may appear less motivated. A certain amount of motivation is essential, but using it as the sole means of selection can result in serious, thoughtful, children being left out. In selection systems where a class teacher works in partnership with an instrument teacher, the class teacher is often in the better position to assess the significance of an individual's motivation.

It is sometimes assumed that motivation towards instrument lessons is a quality that a child either has or lacks. Thus a child who gives up lessons on the violin, for instance, may be deemed to lack motivation, and denied flute lessons. In fact, motivation towards any activity is multi-faceted. In the case of instrument lessons, it is influenced by the instrument chosen, the teacher and style of teaching, the social dynamic of the group of pupils, and so on. In other words, a child who gives up lessons on an instrument is not destined to give up any other instrument that is offered. Amongst a sample of forty-six professional orchestral musicians (Mills, 1985), I found four who had first taken lessons on an orchestral instrument significantly different from the one they were employed to play. A trumpeter and a trombonist had both started with violin lessons. A clarinetist had started with the flute. A tuba player had started with the trombone. In addition, there were some more usual transfers: violinists had become viola players, and cellists had transferred to the double bass. In other words, a decision not to persevere with one instrument does not necessarily imply a general lack of ability to persevere.

5   Think carefully about any assessment you want to make of 'musical ability'

Selection for instruments sometimes includes some form of assessment of 'musical ability'. Often, this is based on the child's ability to sing in tune. This is a highly dubious predictor of any sort of ability. The assessor is really interested in whether the child can 'hear in tune', yet a child who can hear fine differences in pitch may still lack the vocal control to sing a simple song in tune. In other words, a child who sings in tune probably has fine pitch discrimination, but the converse is not true. Other teacher-designed ability tests include aural tests administered from the piano. A teacher may play a chord, and then ask children how many notes it contains, for instance. There are two main problems in this. First, children already familiar with the sound of a piano will be at an advantage. Second, the ability to count the number

165

of notes in a chord is not a major component of performing. To what extent can the teacher be certain that the ability to count the number of notes in a chord is indicative of any more general ability? In other words, to what extent is this test a valid predictor of any wider ability?

How can you avoid these problems? If you wish to include assessment of children's musical ability in your selection procedure, you can use a published test, such as my *Group Tests of Musical Abilities* (Mills, 1988a). Published tests can offer several advantages over home-made tests. First, they may already have been tried out with a large sample of children. Second, an attempt may have been made to minimise the probably inevitable advantage given to children with extensive musical background. Third, the extent to which the tests predict achievement on instruments may have been investigated. Supporting documentation for tests enables you to determine their suitability for your particular purposes.

My view is that children's results in tests should always be interpreted positively. They should not be used to discourage children from taking lessons. The best way of finding out whether a child will benefit from trumpet lessons is to give him some and see what happens. However, test results can lead to your recognition of some able children of whom you were previously unaware. Perhaps they are quiet children who do not customarily make their presence felt at all. Perhaps they are children who have not displayed particular musical behaviour; they could dislike singing, or may not sing in tune. A high-scoring child might be offered some special encouragement to start lessons.

Should all children be tested as a matter of course? I see little purpose in this. But if a decision needs to be made about a child's musical future, a test score can provide a piece of evidence to be considered alongside that which a teacher already has at her disposal.

6   Think carefully about the extent to which you wish to consider factors concerned with home background and academic attainment

It is well known that factors that predispose children towards academic success, such as high measured intelligence and positive parental support, also correlate with musical attainment. Desmond Sergeant and Gillian Thatcher (1974) found that children with high measured intelligence and social status tend to score better in musical ability tests. Because of the tradition of equating effective selection for instrument tuition with *low wastage,* such fortunate children are often given priority when places for instrument lessons are scarce. My view is that this is wrong. There are no perfect correlations between musical attainment and social or academic factors. Some children from the most depressive social circumstances become successful musicians. And there are many professional musicians with few formal academic qualifications. If anything, I would argue for children in less favourable circumstances to be given preferential treatment. They are probably less likely to have parents able or willing to provide instrument lessons outside school. As teachers, we try to provide a primary education that enables children to achieve their potential, regardless of their social background or ability. Why should instrument lessons be any different?

School music and secondary teachers

There was a time when primary/secondary liaison in music was almost unheard of. The range of musical experience of children entering a particular secondary school was often vast. Much of the variation could be attributed to the differing status of music within the feeder, or partner, schools. Some secondary teachers responded imaginatively to the range of initial experience. Others reacted by taking everyone back to what they regarded as the beginning, thus boring some children through repetition. A further group organised class music as a form of entertainment, rather than a progressive course. Primary schools and secondary schools viewed themselves as autonomous; nothing much happened to remedy mismatch, or to find a more constructive way of dealing with it.

With falling rolls, and more positive attitudes to primary/ secondary liaison, secondary music teachers have sometimes found themselves with some time available to teach in one or more of their partner schools. Unfortunately, this sort of teaching has sometimes been a hit-and run, top-down, affair, with secondary teachers arriving to teach primary children whatever it is that the secondary teacher wants them to know when they change school. The content of these secondary teachers' lessons was not always related to anything else that the children were doing, and was sometimes conveyed in a specialist way almost guaranteed to intimidate every primary teacher without a music degree. At its worst, this style of liaison actually decreased the amount of music teaching and learning taking place in the primary school.

Thanks partly to the publication of *Music from 5 to 16* (DES, 1985a), and also the introduction of the National Curriculum, there is now much greater awareness that music in school is, at the very least, a 5 to 16 process. This has opened the door to more constructive pooling of the staffing of secondary and primary schools. Primary and secondary teachers learn from each other. Though secondary music teachers, as trained music specialists, often have more in the way of formal music qualifications, there is often much they can learn about music education from primary teachers and children: the high expectations that can be set, the almost general enthusiasm for music of primary children, the possibilities of informal modes of teaching, the relationship between music and the remainder of the curriculum, and so on.

With the introduction of the National Curriculum in music in 1992, primary/secondary liaison takes on new relevance. More than ever before, secondary teachers need to find out about the musical achievements of their intake, so that they can build on them. They can acquire much information from reports for children who are completing Year 6. But first-hand observation, too, is helpful. Seeing and hearing primary children at work helps secondary teachers set expectations that are high enough, and enusre that the secondary curriculum reinforces, and does not simply repeat, the primary curriculum. Sadly, secondary teachers are more likely to under-estimate than over-estimate work they have not seen. That does children no good, and does not add to the musical reputation of the primary school.

Secondary music teachers sometimes have more time in the second half of the summer term, when their GCSE (and possibly A-level) candidates have left school. Perhaps you could invite them – once your SATS are over – to join your children composing, singing and playing, and encourage them to discuss some children's reports and recordings with the children themselves.

A school staff for music

A school staff for music includes all the teachers: consultants, generalists, visiting teachers, the headteacher. It may also include secondary teachers, parents, and other members of the community. Though a music curriculum leader may take prime responsibility for writing a music curriculum document, everyone is involved in its design and implementation.

Teachers have individual differences in their musical interests. No two teachers working in the same school will interpret their school music curriculum document in exactly the same way. The best sort of music curriculum document secures progression whilst capitalising on the diversity of teachers' musical experience.

One year, a child may be in the class of a teacher who chooses to play and perform a lot of rap. The next year, there may be more Ravel. The year after, it may be mainly ragtime. One year, most singing may be unaccompanied. The next year, the piano may be used more. The third year may be the year of the guitar. A teacher who is a visual artist may favour the use of visual stimuli for composing, whereas another teacher may make more extensive use of poetry. The mathematics curriculum leader may place emphasis on pattern in music. The PE specialist may see close links between music and dance. Another teacher may feel more comfortable teaching music as a self-contained subject. Some teachers will have strong personal musical interests which they want to share with children. Others will prefer to start by considering the music that children bring with them from their community, or the musical ideas conveyed by the school or home environment. This range of interest and emphasis is a source of great strength to a school. A staff that is able to pool all this can offer children a music programme much richer than one person could ever supply. Children continually become aware of new dimensions of music, and new emphases within music making. They have first-hand experience of the co-existence of different musical traditions, and plenty of material from which to develop their personal musical taste.

Within a school staff for music, teachers can be encouraged to develop and build on their musical strengths. They also learn from each other. Consultants help generalist teachers to develop as music teachers. In return, they learn much from those they help. By finding approaches to teaching that generalists feel ready to tackle, the consultants develop their own repertoire of teaching skills. Through teaching generalists music skills, consultants become better equipped to teach them to children. Very few adults who are fluent music readers, for instance, can remember learning to read music themselves. Teaching an adult learner who is able to articulate his or her difficulties can sometimes lead to a more consistent approach with children. But there is also much more to be learnt from generalists: the differing

169

responses of individuals to the same piece of music, the open response of teachers who have not come to view some sorts of music as 'good' and others as 'bad', a way of talking about music that is free of technical jargon. Music teaching is a co-operative enterprise in which children gain from teachers, and teachers gain from each other.

Notes

Chapter 1

1 (p. 3) In the Primary Survey (DES, 1978), HMI found that 40% of 7-year-olds, 50% of 9-year-olds and 55% of 11-year-olds were taught music by someone other than their class teacher. More recently, HMI (DES, 1985b) found that only about 40% of teachers of junior children in combined and middle schools teach any music. In both surveys, there is no other subject in which fewer children are taught by their class teacher.

2 (p. 3) In a survey of the opinions of 465 primary teachers, the Primary Schools Research and Development Group (1983) found that 26.6% of teachers think there is little need for all teachers to be able to teach music. 19.6% of teachers think there is little need for all teachers to be competent in Religious Education. The percentages given for all other subjects are substantially lower.

3 (p. 3) According to a series of HMI surveys (DES, 1978, 1982, 1985b), around 80% of primary schools of at least moderate size have a teacher with special curriculum responsibility for music. No other subject has more teachers with special responsibility.

4 (p. 3) Analysis of references to subjects in advertisements for main scale primary posts in *The Times Educational Supplement* over various periods during the 1980s has consistently shown more mention of music than any other subject. Interestingly, music remained the most sought-after subject strength in an analysis I carried out over a three-week period in the spring of 1989, a time when one might have expected primary schools to be attempting to develop their subject strengths in mathematics, English and science, in anticipation of the introduction of the National Curriculum in these subjects at Key Stage 1 in September 1989.

Chapter 2

1 (p. 13) *Switch* is in *Pompaleerie Jig* (D. Thompson and K. Baxter, 1978, published by Arnold-Wheaton) and *Conductor* is in *Sounds Fun* (T. Wishart, 1975, published by Schools Council Publications).

2 (p. 18) I do not mind if a piece I am conducting ends up with no discernible pulse. Such a piece is sometimes described as a *soundscape*. But leaders who, at least initially, do not feel comfortable with this sort of piece, can often engineer a pulse by choosing, as their first performer, a child who produces a regular, and loud, sound. Performers who enter later will usually fit in with this pulse.

3 (p. 21) Determining the details of the music we compose by the throw of a die is not as unmusical as it might at first seem. Some twentieth-century composers have employed chance procedures in their compositions. For example, some of the material in John Cage's *Music of Changes* for piano (1951) was determined by the toss of a coin.

Chapter 3

1 (p. 23) In *improvising*, the composing and performing take place at the same time; the performer composes as she or he goes along. *Arranging* consists of adapting another composition. Thus a composer might make a piano arrangement of a folk melody, or of a work by Handel.

2 (p. 26) An account of the development of song in pre-school children can be found in *The Developmental Psychology of Music* by David J. Hargreaves (1986).

3 (p. 27) Xylophones have wooden bars, whereas metallophones and glockenspiels have metal ones. However, toy manufacturers, as opposed to musical instrument manufacturers, are not all clear about this. The fact that toy 'xylophones' sometimes have plastic or metal bars causes some children and teachers to become confused.

4 (p. 41) John Paynter (1972) *The Space Dragon of Galatar*, Universal Edition.

5 (p.46) Any five-note scale (e.g. C D E F G, C D E F G) is pentatonic. The pentatonic scale referred to here (C D E G A) can be transposed to start on any note to give, for instance, F G A C D or G A B D E or all the piano *black* notes: F♯ G♯ A♯ C♯ D♯.

6 (p. 46) The semitone (e.g. the interval B–C, or C–C♯), is both the smallest, and most dissonant, interval in the Western scale. The lack of dissonance of intervals drawn from the pentatonic scale C D E G A stems from the absence of single semitone intervals within the scale. The intervals C–D, D–E and G–A consist of two semitones, that is, one tone, and the intervals E–G and A–C consist

172

of three semitones. Most pentatonic scales found in European folk song do not include single semitone intervals.

Chapter 4

1 (p. 56) This poem can be found, for example, in *The Golden Treasury of Poetry*, L. Untermeyer (1961), Collins, London, page 94.

2 (p. 58) An octave is the closest interval between two notes with the same letter name, for example C. See also chapter 7, note 3 (page 174).

3 (p. 59) A *descant* is a second part which lies mainly above the melody. For example, think of descants to Christmas carols.

4 (p. 59) An *ostinato* (plural *ostinati*) is a short melodic or rhythmic phrase which can be repeated as an accompaniment to a substantial section of a melody. Here, HMI are referring particularly to melodic ostinati. For example, try accompanying *Frère Jacques* by repeating just the opening phrase – 'Frère Jacques' – as an ostinato all the way through.

5 (p. 59) A round is a melody which can be performed in two or more parts simply by starting different groups at suitable regularly spaced intervals. *London's Burning* and *Three Blind Mice* are both rounds. Every round is a canon. But canons may be more freely organised. For instance, the parts may not come in at equal intervals of time, or they may enter on different notes, or proceed at a different pace. In *Old Abram Brown* (see *Flying a Round* (Gadsby and Harrop, 1982, A & C Black)), for instance, a second part could sing at a half, or even a quarter, the pace of the first part.

6 (p. 66) *The Runaway Train*, by Carson Robison and Robert E. Massey, is in *Hullabaloo-balay*, published by Macmillan, 1988.

7 (p. 69) A drone accompaniment consists of a single low note (or possibly a single low chord) which is sustained throughout the melody.

8 (p. 69) How can you work this out? Melodies nearly always end with their key note, so sing the song through, starting on an E, and check that it finishes on a C. It is safer still to take the key from the chord you would use to accompany the final note. Check that the chord of C makes sense with the final note of this song by playing it on an instrument such as an electronic keyboard. Published songs often have chord symbols written above the music; try taking the final chord as your key chord. Just occasionally, for instance when a song moves through several keys, this system breaks down. This is rare amongst songs in children's songbooks.

9 (p. 69) Each line of *Three Blind Mice* can be repeated to form a melodic accompaniment because the song is a round. With other songs, judge by ear whether or not this approach is successful.

10 (p. 70) To establish the pace at which you should sing *Frère Jacques* to fit with *Three Blind Mice*, note that the rhythm of 'dormez-vous?' is the same as that of 'three blind mice'.

11 (p. 70) Try, for instance, repeating the melodic phrase 'Frère Jacques, three blind mice' (C D E C, E D C).

Chapter 7

1 (p. 111) For instance, Igaga and Versey (1977, 1978) compared the rhythmic abilities of Ugandan and English children.

2 (p. 112) Many lateralisation studies involve only right-handed subjects. As Shuter-Dyson and Gabriel (1981) point out, the cerebral organisation of left-handers is sometimes even less straightforward.

3 (p. 119) Choose any note on the piano. Find the closest note to the immediate right or left which is at the same point in the pattern of black or white notes. These two notes will have the same letter-name. Play them together, and you have an octave chord. It is generally agreed that an octave chord is relatively hard to distinguish from a single note.

Examples of octaves.

4 (p. 119) In guitar notation, the symbol D is used to denote the chord D major, the symbol G is used to denote the chord G major, and so on.

5 (p. 119) However, there is no great mystery to this. Such matters are best taught live, not through a book. Ask a friend or colleague for help.

174

Chapter 8

1 (p. 133) *Prehistoric Ramble* is in *40 Music Games to Make and Play* (Tillman, 1983, Macmillan).

2 (p. 134) *Ticking Clocks* is in *Flying a Round* (Gadsby and Harrop, 1982, A & C Black).

3 (p. 136) *Passar al Fuoco i di quieti e contenti mentre la pioggio fuor bagna ben cento* is translated on one record sleeve as 'The day is spent in peace and serenity at the fire, while the rain drizzles down'.

4 (p. 139) In *The Arts in Schools* (CGF, 1982), these activities were named 'participation' and 'appreciation'.

Chapter 9

1 (p. 159) The correlation between achievement on brass instruments and appropriateness of mouthpiece size is only small ($r = 0.28 \pm 0.088$). The correlation between finger length and achievement on the violin is lower still ($r = 0.17 \pm 0.09$). In fact it is much the same as the violinists' result for teeth-evenness – not a characteristic we would expect to be relevant to violinists!

2 (p. 160) Some of the instrumentalists were students at a specialist music school. The remainder were receiving professional training as musicians.

3 (p. 163) Occasionally, one finds a piece of music that is not playable by both men and women. In Luciano Berio's *Sequenza V*, written for solo trombone in 1966, the trombonist has to sing notes outside the female vocal range into his trombone. The existence of this piece is not enough to render the trombone only suitable for men, as many successful women trombonists have shown.

4 (p. 163) Leontiev (1969), amongst others, has shown that pitch discrimination is often more accurate within the vocal range, because of the possibility of sub-vocalisation. Thus, it might be argued that men are likely to play low instruments better in tune. Yet Leontiev showed that ability to discriminate pitch finely within the vocal range could be extended beyond it. I am sure that I am not alone in finding that my ability to tune children's cellos, for instance, has improved with practice.

References

Abeles, H.F. and Porter, S.Y. (1978) 'The sex-stereotyping of musical instruments', *Journal of Research in Music Education*, **26** (2), 65–75.

Addison, R. (1988) 'Beyond music' in Salaman, W. and Mills, J. (eds), *Challenging Assumptions: New Perspectives in the Education of Music Teachers*, University of Exeter School of Education.

Arnold, D. (1983) *The New Oxford Companion to Music*, Oxford University Press.

Association of Professional Music Therapists (1988) *Music Therapy in the Education Service: a Consultation Document*, APMT.

Bentley, A. (1966) *Musical Ability in Children and its Measurement*, Harrap, London.

Bentley, A. (1968) *'Monotones' – a Comparison with 'Normal' Singers*, Novello, London.

Ben-Tovim, A. and Boyd, D. (1985) *The Right Instrument for Your Child*, Gollancz, London.

Betjeman, J. (1960) *Summoned by Bells*, John Murray, London.

Bridger, W.H. (1961) 'Sensory habituation and discrimination in the human neonate', *American Journal of Psychiatry*, **117**, 991–96.

Bryant, P. and Bradley, L. (1985) *Children's Reading Problems*, Blackwell, Oxford.

Buckton, R. (1988) 'Vocal accuracy of young children – a New Zealand survey' in Kemp, A. (ed.) *Research in Music Education: a Festschrift for Arnold Bentley*, International Society for Music Education.

Bulman, B. (1987) 'Music: the developing experience', *Special Children*, March, 8–11.

Bunting, R. (1977) 'The common language of music', *Music in the Secondary School Curriculum*, Working paper 6, Schools Council, York University.

Cage, J. (1968) *Silence: Letters and Writings*, Calder and Boyars, London.

Calouste Gulbenkian Foundation (1982) *The Arts in Schools: Principles, Practice and Provision*, Calouste Gulbenkian Foundation.

Central Advisory Council for Education (England) (1967) *Children and their Primary Schools* (Plowden Report), HMSO, London.

Cleall, C. (1970) *Voice Production in Choral Technique*, Novello, London.

Cooper, D. (1985) 'Selection procedures used by peripatetic instrumental teachers', *British Journal of Music Education*, 2 (1), 19–38.

Cornford, F.M. (1969) *The Republic of Plato*, Oxford University Press.

Corredor, J.M. (1956) *Conversations with Casals*, Hutchinson, London.

Crowther, R. and Durkin, K. (1982) 'Research overview: language in music education', *Psychology of Music*, 10 (1), 59–60.

Curriculum Council for Wales (1992) *Music in the National Curriculum Non-Statutory Guidance for Teachers*.

Davies, C. (1986) 'Say it till a song comes (reflections on songs invented by children 3–13)', *British Journal of Music Education*, 3 (3), 279–93.

Davies, J.B. (1978) *The Psychology of Music*, Hutchinson, London.

Department of Education and Science (now Department for Education) (1978) *Primary Education in England: a Survey by HM Inspectors of Schools*

(1982) *Education 5 to 9: An Illustrative Survey of 80 First Schools in England*

(1985a) *Curriculum Matters 4: Music from 5 to 16*

(1985b) *Education 8 to 12 in Combined and Middle Schools*

(1985c) *GCSE – The National Criteria – Music*

(1989) *National Curriculum: From Policy to Practice*

(1995) The National Curriculum (England)
HMSO, London.

Gardner, H. and Winner, E. (1982) 'First intimations of artistry' in Strauss, S. and Stavy, R. (eds) *U-shaped Behavioural Growth*, Academic Press, New York.

Griswold, P.A. and Chroback, D.A. (1981) 'Sex-role associations of music instruments and occupations by gender and major', *Journal of Research in Music Education*, **29** (1), 57–62.

Hargreaves, D.J. (1986) *The Developmental Psychology of Music*, Cambridge University Press.

Igaga, J.M. and Versey, J. (1977) 'Cultural differences in rhythmic perception', *Psychology of Music*, **5** (1), 23–27.

(1978) 'Cultural differences in rhythmic performance', *Psychology of Music*, **6** (1), 61–64.

Jones, F.W. (1941) *The Principles of Anatomy as Seen in the Hand*, Ballière and Cox, London.

Keller, H. (1987) *Criticism*, Faber and Faber, London.

Kemp, A. (1981) 'The personality structure of the musician: 1. Identifying a profile of traits for the performer', *Psychology of Music*, **9** (1), 3–14.

Lamp, C. and Keys, N. (1935) 'Can aptitude for specific instruments be predicted?', *American Journal of Educational Psychology*, **26**, 587–96.

Leontiev, A.N. (1969) 'On the biological and social aspects of human development: the training of auditory ability' in Cole, M. and Matzman, I. (eds) *A Handbook of Contemporary Soviet Psychology*, Basic Books, New York.

Letwin, O. (1987) 'Testing issues', *The Times Educational Supplement*, 18 September, 112.

Loane, B. (1984) 'Thinking about children's composition', *British Journal of Music Education*, **1** (3), 205–32.

Malbran, S. and Furno, S. (1987) 'Objective test for songs', *Bulletin of the Council for Research in Music Education*, **91**, 110–18.

Marshall, S. (1963) *An Experiment in Education*, Cambridge University Press.

Mawbey, W.E. (1973) 'Wastage from instrumental classes in school', *Psychology of Music*, **1** (1), 33–43.

Mills, J.

(1983) *Identifying Potential Orchestral Musicians*, D.Phil. thesis, University of Oxford.

(1984) 'The "Pitch" subtest of Bentley's "Measures of Musical Abilities": a test from the 1960s reconsidered in the 1980s', *Psychology of Music*, **12** (2), 94–105.

(1985) 'Gifted instrumentalists: how can we recognise them?', *British Journal of Music Education*, **2** (1), 39–49.

(1988a) *Group Tests of Musical Abilities: Teacher's Guide and Recorded Test*, NFER-Nelson, Windsor.

(1988b) 'Tips for teachers as traps: an example from instrumental tuition' in Salaman, W. and Mills, J. (eds) *Challenging Assumptions: New Perspectives in the Education of Music Teachers*, University of Exeter School of Education.

(1989a) 'The generalist primary teacher of music: a problem of confidence', *British Journal of Music Education*, **6** (2), 125–38.

(1989b) 'Developing listening through composing', *Music Teacher*, March, 9–11.

Moog, H. (1976) *The Musical Experience of the Pre-School Child* (translated by Claudia Clarke), Schott, London.

Morley, T. (1952) *A Plaine and Easie Introduction to Practicalle Musicke*, edited by R.A. Harman, Dent, London.

National Curriculum Council (1989) *A Framework for the Primary Curriculum*

(1992) *Music Non-Statutory Guidance*
National Curriculum Council, York.

Opie, I. and Opie, P. (1985) *The Singing Game*, Oxford University Press.

Paynter, J. (1982) *Music in the Secondary School Curriculum*, Cambridge University Press.

Piaget, J. (1951) *Play, Dreams and Imitation in Childhood*, Routledge and Kegan Paul, London.

Primary Schools Research and Development Group (1983) *Curriculum Responsibility and the Use of Teacher Expertise in the Primary School*, University of Birmingham School of Education.

Robinson, K. (1989) 'The future of the arts in schools?', *The Arts in Schools Project Newsletter 10*, National Curriculum Council.

Ross, M. (1984) *The Aesthetic Impulse*, Pergamon Press, Oxford.

Salaman, W. (1988) 'Personalities in world music education, No. 7 – John Paynter', *International Journal of Music Education*, **12**, 28–32.

Seashore, C.E. (1938) *The Psychology of Music*, McGraw-Hill, London.

Sergeant, D.C. and Thatcher, G. (1974) 'Intelligence, social status, and musical abilities', *Psychology of Music*, **2** (2), 32–57.

Shuter-Dyson, R. and Gabriel, C. (1981) *The Psychology of Musical Ability*, Methuen, London.

Swanwick, K.
  (1979) *A Basis for Music Education*, NFER-Nelson, Windsor.

  (1988) *Music, Mind, and Education*, Routledge, London.

Swanwick, K. and Tillman, J. (1986) 'The sequence of musical development: a study of children's composition', *British Journal of Music Education*, **3** (3), 305–339.

Taylor, S. (1973) 'Musical development of children aged seven to eleven', *Psychology of Music*, **1** (1), 44–49.

Tillman, J. (1988) 'Music in the primary school and the national curriculum' in Salaman, W. and Mills, J. (eds) *Challenging Assumptions: New Perspectives in the Education of Music Teachers*, University of Exeter School of Education.

Vulliamy, G. and Lee, E. (1976) *Pop Music in School*, Cambridge University Press.

Welch, G. (1979) 'Vocal range and poor pitch singing', *Psychology of Music*, **7** (2), 13–31.

Welsh Office (1995) Music in the National Curriculum (Wales), HMSO, London.

Wisbey, A.
  (1980) *Music as the Source of Learning*, MTP, Lancaster.

  (1981) *Learn to Sing to Learn to Read*, British Broadcasting Corporation, London.

Index

This is not an exhaustive index; it lists definitions and passages that cannot be readily located through scanning of the Contents pages.